CHANDI PURANA

Chandi Purana

A GODDESS GOES TO WAR

SARALA DAS

General Editor
UDAYANATH SAHOO

Translated by
BASANT KUMAR TRIPATHY

with an introduction by
URMISHREE BEDAMATTA

ADIKABI SARALA DAS
CHAIR OF ODIA STUDIES
Jawaharlal Nehru University,
New Delhi

MANOHAR
2026

This book is the English version of *Chandi Purana*, written in Odia by Sarala Das, edited by Prof. Krushna Charan Sahoo (1929–97) and published by Books and Books, Binodbihari, Cuttack, 1984.

First published 2022
Reprinted 2025, 2026

ISBN 978-93-91928-09-4

Published by
Adikabi Sarala Das Chair of Odia Studies
Jawaharlal Nehru University,
New Delhi 110 067
&
Ajay Kumar Jain *for*
Manohar Publishers & Distributors
4753/23 Ansari Road, Daryaganj
New Delhi 110 002

Printed at
Replika Press Pvt. Ltd.

Contents

Foreword 7

A Goddess Goes to War: Claiming the Right to Modesty *An Introduction to the Odia Legend of Chandi* 13

1. Prayer to Sri Ganesh 33
2. Prayer to Goddess Sarala 35
3. Mahisasura's Meditation 37
4. Mahisasura's Conquest of Kurancheka 48
5. Mahisasura's Battle with Merusula 51
6. Dhumralochana Ordained as a Charioteer 53
7. Mahisasura Concedes Defeat to Chanda and Munda 55
8. Mahisasura's Marriage with Chandrabati 62
9. Mahisasura's Conquest of Jambu Island 70
10. Mahisasura's Battle with Shumbha and Nishumbha 76
11. Mahisasura Loses the Battle 85

12. Mahisasura's Letter to Indra 89
13. Durga's Stay at Ratnagiri 111
14. Mahisasura Informed of Durga's Arrival 118
15. The Killing of Chanda and Munda 124
16. The Killing of Shumbha and Nishumbha 128
17. The Killing of Chamara and Bemala 135
18. The Killing of Kantimala, Raktabirjya, Biraghanta, Kaladanda and Bidulaksha 139
19. The Tale of Bailochana 160
20. The Demon Commanders Challenge Durga 168
21. Mahisasura Proceeds to the Battlefield 196
22. The Killing of Kalabimochana 200
23. The Killing of Mahisasura 208
Glossary 237

Foreword

Adikabi Sarala Das Chair of Odia Studies started its activities at the Jawaharlal Nehru University (JNU) with the financial help of Government of Odisha from 26 December 2017 in the Centre of Indian Languages (CIL), School of Language, Literature and Culture Studies (SLL&CS). The Chair intends to represent Odisha, its language, literature and culture in all its multilingual and pluralistic manifestations. The Chair encourages comparative studies across a wide range of domains and also aims at disseminating knowledge of Odia language, literature and culture both at the national and international levels.

After the successful launch of the translation of *Bichitra Ramayana*, a fifteenth-century classic, in 2020, we are now bringing out our second ambitious project in print, the English version of the *Chandi Purana*, composed by Adikabi Sarala Das in Odia language. It retells one of the greatest themes of Indian mythology dealing with the heroic exploits of Goddess Durga — how she outwitted and eliminated the demon king Mahisasura and his powerful commanders. The battle between Durga and Mahishasura is considered to be more violent and more destructive than those of the *Ramayana* and the *Mahabharata*, which is elaborately narrated in texts such as the *Durga Saptasati*, the *Kalika Purana*, the *Markandeya Purana*, *Devi Bhagavata*, the *Vishnu Purana*, etc. Referring to the source of his work, Sarala proclaims: I'm narrating to you the *Vishnu Purana* which is the essence of the *Bhagavata*.

Sarala's literary excellence, however, does not lie in producing the Odia version of a story of the long past written in Sanskrit. His objective is three-fold: (1) to create a habitation of knowledge by converting, rather subverting the subject to accommodate the local religious beliefs and customs, (2) to transmit the new knowledge system to the common folk whom he is writing for by using legends and folklore and (3) to break free from the Sanskrit – Prakrit tradition and reset it into an indigenous literary culture.

In *Chandi Purana*, Durga is equated with Sarala Chandi of Kanakapur in eastern Odisha. She is said to be the daughter of the first Brahma, Krupajal. Banished by her father for a minor offence she took shelter in Chandrabhaga (near Konark) bearing the name Hingula and later she came to Kanakapura where she is being worshipped as Sarala Chandi for thousands of years. She conforms to the Odia legend of Chandi and one of Vishnu's incarnations. Second, in all other texts the retelling of the story of Durga is conducted by Sage Medha for the benefit of king Suratha and Samadhi Vaishya who had been turned out of their respective positions by those whom they loved best. Sarala changes the narrator and the listener and turns the affair of retelling to an elaborate conversation between Sage Shuka and king Parikshit. Here Sage Shuka retells the story to king Parikshit, who, under a curse, is bitten by Takshaka and waiting for his imminent death. Here Durga is not only a Vaishnavi, but also one of the incarnations of Lord Vishnu. We see the goddess sitting on the Vinchyagiri with a veil over her head, which is a typical picture of a village woman in Odisha. She is portrayed less as a goddess and more as a symbol of eternal womanhood.

First, to bring the subject within the domain of the local religion, Sarala adopts the theories of subversion and mutation. Sanskrit, however, is not a unified language and the texts written in it cannot be called standardized ones as there might be many texts on the same subject in other languages, nearly as old as Sanskrit. Therefore, there is always a space for modification and variation, a space for intertextuality. Sarala Das declares himself as an unschooled Shudra farmer who has no access to the world of *shastras*. He owes a deep sense of gratitude to Sarala Chandi, who, as he says, used to narrate the *shastras* to him during her nightly visitations, which he puts in words as soon as the Sun rises. His unflinching devotion to her is expressed when he says, 'I'm Sarala Das, son of Sarala Chandi/Krupajal's daughter.'

Sarala's presentation of Durga's character and conduct is not based on her role as a goddess or as a warrior only; more than anything else, he views her as a graceful woman of the earth, sometimes a symbol of 'Indian femininity'. She adds new dimensions to the war story, which is the man-woman relationship. She explains herself '. . . we are not the kind of women you think us to be. As mother/we bring you to the earth; as wives/we spend nights with you; as Kalika we kill you/and, as fire, we burn you after you die/you've beginning and end, but we've only the middle/we create and destroy.' In an answer to Mahisa's commanders who treat women with slights and barbs, she passes a note of caution, saying, '. . . we represent/ the eternal motherhood; we're yoginis/the symbols of purity'. It is the sight of her nakedness that brings an end to Mahisa's life, not the weapons.

Second, to communicate the new knowledge system to the common folk, Sarala administers legends and folklore into the text. It is well known that Durga is born from the fire emanated from the anger of the panicked gods who have been driven away from their heavenly abode by Mahisasura. Her forehead was made by Brahma's fire, face by Narayan, teeth by Maheswar, eyes by fire, nose by Indra, radiance by Aditya, tongue by moon, cheeks by Yama, chest by Kuber, armpit by Nirakar, navel by Sanaka, folds on her abdomen by Ashwini Kumar, thighs by Prajapati, feet by Ananta Vasuki, toes by nine planets and Bhrugu, fingers by *Kunda* buds, back by Hemavanta, hair by stars, belly by Varuna, water in her body by Rain, one thousand hands by forty-nine winds, words by Yama and holiness by Vaishnavas. After she emerged from fire, some of the gods offered her weapons, others clothes and ornaments. Peculiar enough, Sarala adds two more contributors, one from the human world, another from the kingdom of animals. Arundhati teaches the goddess the *gauri sauri* method of cooking (cooking without cutting the vegetables and adding no spices). The idea behind it may be to make the goddess's life as a woman complete. Second, the pangolin offers the goddess its skin, too thick to penetrate. Another example of innovation is that Sarala portrays Arundhati as the daughter of a *chandal* whom Basistha marries under duress. Under the spiritual influence of Basistha, she later becomes one of the deities of heaven. The upward mobility of the low born shows Sarala's social concern. His message here is loud and clear that caste does not determine one's position in the society.

Sarala wrote during a period, when Odia language did not have an independent identity; it was reeling under the influence of Sanskrit and Prakrit. It was only during his time that Odia became the state language and received the patronage of Odia kings. Sarala's works reveal a continuous effort by the poet to break from the Sanskrit-Prakrit tradition and form an indigenous literary culture. He tried to give a distinct shape to the native language, not only by writing for the natives, but also by expressing his thoughts with the language they spoke. The folk elements in his works are plenty, bringing his art closer to the readers.

In localising the master text, Sarala breaks the *shastrik* and *brahmanical* mould of the earlier texts and forms a new kind of literature that is indigenous, secular and democratic. He was the first poet to take Odia language from orality to literarization. His works such as the *Bichitra Ramayana*, the *Mahabharata* and the *Chandi Purana* usher in a new age as the first epics written by an unschooled Shudra poet of the fifteenth century. He imbibed his works with the hopes and aspirations and the way of life of the commoners. He set new cannons which went a long way in developing Odia literature. He deliberately calls his work *Purana*. He specified the genre to ground readers' expectations at the outset, that a reader should expect a local *Chandi Purana* and not merely a work of translation or imitation.

On this occasion I express my sincere thanks to Prof. Basant Kumar Tripathy for undertaking the translation of this landmark volume into English and to Dr. Urmishree Bedamatta for providing us with a brilliant piece of Introduction. I am also thankful to Sri Ajay Kumar Jain of Manohar Publishers and Distributors, New Delhi for taking the onerous task of publishing the translation of the classical text of Odia literature jointly with Adikabi Sarala Das Chair of Odia Studies at CIL/SLL&CS, Jawaharlal Nehru University.

PROF. UDAYANATH SAHOO
Adikabi Sarala Das Chair of Odia Studies
Centre of Indian languages
School of Language, Literature & Culture studies
Jawaharlal Nehru University
New Delhi-110067

A Goddess Goes to War: Claiming the Right to Modesty

An Introduction to the Odia Legend of Chandi

The young modern reader of the Odia *Chandi Purana* (*ChP* henceforth) is far removed from the empirical, social and imaginative realm of its author Sarala Das, so much so that the distance might lead to a catastrophic misunderstanding of the actual nature of the text. What kind of modern reader do we wish to imply? A brilliantly creative reader[1] who looks for stories to retell and wants to be read? Is it a scholar[2]

[1] My reference is to Anuja Chandramouli, the author of *Shakti: The Divine Feminine* (New Delhi: Rupa, 2015). Chandramouli's book provides a witty insight into the complex character of women and enjoys a wide appeal among young readers.

[2] Such scholars are numerous but some noteworthy names are Thomas B. Coburn, Cheever MacKenzie Brown, J.A.B. van Buitenen, M. Haraprasad Shastri, R.C. Hazra, F.E. Pargiter, Ludo Rocher, and P.V. Kane, who continue to be cited by contemporary scholars of Puranic literature. The *pancalaksana* of *sarga* (stories about the origin of the universe), *pratisarga* (dissolution of the universe and its recreation), *vamsa* (genealogies of devas, asuras, rishis and kings), *manvantara* (a cosmic cycle of Creation which is

whose preoccupation is the study of the five identifiers (*pancalaksana*) of the Puranic genre of literature and the incongruences in this body of literature? Such scholarly work has yielded one important observation though, that although the subject of Purana is ancient, it is still new.[3] Is it a scholar[4] whose preoccupation is the study of Puranas as

---

presided by a Manu, the progenitor of mankind), and *vamsanucharita* (stories of the rise and fall of clans and dynasties) which were posited for the first time by Amarasimha (fifth-sixth centuries) in *Amarakosa*, may be taken as broad identifiers, for scholars have not been able to identify any extant Purana except the *Vishnu Purana* and the *Bhagavata Purana* which completely satisfy these conditions. In this context, see Stephan Hillyer Levitt, 'A Note on the Compound *Pancalaksana* in Amarasinha's *Namalinganusasana*', in *Purana*, vol. XVIII, no. 1, Varanasi: Bulletin of the Purana Department, All India Kashiraj Trust, 1976: 5–38). Sarala Das's *Chandi Purana* has only *vamsa*. Important scholarly works on the *pancalaksana* include R.C. Hazra's 'The Aswamedha, the Common Source of Origin of the Purana Panca-Laksana and the Mahabharata', in *Annals of the Bhandarkar Oriental Research Institute*, vol. 36, no. 4, Pune: Bhandarkar Oriental Research Institute, 1955: 190–203 and Willibald Kirfel's *Das Purana Pancalaksana* (Bonn: Kurt Shroeder, 1927). For a history of scholarship on the *pancalaksana*, see Ludo Rocher, '*Puranam Pancalaksanam* in "The Puranas", 24–30', in Jan Gonda (ed.), *A History of Indian Literature*, vol. II, Fasc. 3, Weisbaden: Otto Harrassowitz, 1986.

[3] It would be helpful to do a simultaneous reading of F.E. Pargiter's *Ancient Indian Historical Tradition* (London: Oxford University Press, 1922), and Giorgio Bonazzoli's 'The Dynamic Canon of the Puranas', in *Purana*, vol. XXI, no. 2, Varanasi: Bulletin of the Purana Department, All India Kashiraj Trust, 1979: 116–66. While Pargiter argues that a history of ancient India ought to be built not only on the Vedas and Vedic literature but also on the Puranic and epic tradition, Bonazzoli explains the origin and evolution of the Purana tradition itself. For a very brief overview of Puranas, see R.C. Hazra's 'The Puranas', in Haridass Bhattacharya (ed.), *The Cultural Heritage of India*, vol. 2 (Calcutta: Ramakrishna Mission Institute of Culture, 1962: 246-7).

[4] Of relevance in this area of scholarship are Rachel Fell McDermott's *Singing to the Goddess: Poems to Kali and Uma from Bengal* (Oxford: Oxford

sectarian manifestos of religion and rituals? Such approach makes us think of a casing as Sakta literature for *ChP* alongside other texts such as Bana's *Candisataka*, *Devi Mahatmya*, *Devi Bhagavata Purana* and *Kalika Purana*.[5] Yet others, inspired by methods of textual criticism, have sought to focus on the historicity of the Puranas,[6] a debate yet to be settled with any

---

University Press, 2001) and Hillary Rodrigues's *Ritual Worship of the Great Goddess: The Liturgy of the Durga Puja with Interpretations* (Albany: SUNY Press, 2003). *The Magic of Kali. Encountering Kali* (California: University of California Press, 2003), a book edited by Rachel Fell McDermott and Jeffrey J. Kripal helped me get a bird's-eye view of multicultural perspectives on the Goddess Kali. Stella Kramrisch's 'The Indian Great Goddess', in *History of Religions*, vol. 14, no. 4, Chicago: University of Chicago Press, 1975: 235–65 recounts certain myths of the Goddess to show the polyvalence in the image of the great Goddess. David Kinsley's *Tantric Visions of the Divine Feminine* (New Delhi: Motilal Banarsidass, 1998) dwells on the different archetypal but 'forbidden' forms of the devi which awaken aspects of our consciousness.

[5] My point of emphasis here is the Sakta corpus in both Sanskritic and Bhasha traditions. David Shulman does a reading of the Tamil versions of the Mahisamardini story in 'The Murderous Bride: Tamil Versions of the Myth of Devi and the Buffalo-Demon', in *History of Religions*, vol. 16, no. 2, Chicago: University of Chicago Press, 1976: 120–46.

[6] For debates in this regard, I have depended on A. Berriedale Keith's 'The Age of the Puranas', in *The Journal of the Royal Asiatic Society of Great Britain and Ireland*, Cambridge: Cambridge University Press, 1914: 1021–32 and 'Dating the Puranas', in Ludo Rocher's, *The Puranas*, Connecticut: American Oriental Society, pp. 100–3. As far as the origin of the image of Mahisamardini (the slayer of Mahisa) is concerned, iconography research dates it as far back as the Kusana period (first to fourth century; in this context, see J.C. Harle's 'On a Disputed Element in the Iconography of Early Mahisasuramardini Images' in *Ars Orientalis*, vol. 8, The Smithsonian Institution and the Department of of the History of Art, University of Michigan 1970: 147–53'. The earliest textual representation of the image perhaps is Banabhatta's *Candisataka* (seventh century) which G.P. Quackenbos says, is 'alleged to be a rival poem to the *Suryasataka*' which was written by the Sanskrit poet Mayura (see 'Preface', in *The Sanskrit Poems*

degree of finality. And, of course, given the title of the text, there has been enough stretching to emphasize its feminist or anti-feminist implications.[7] It would be worthwhile, then, to draw the young modern reader to the evocative power of *ChP* actualized through imagery, meaning and emotion.[8] However, it would not be easy to get such a reader interested in the text unless it speaks to individual concerns about the scope and possibility of making life choices under specific conditions.

ChP is an original abridgement by Sarala Das who, in full awareness of the 'Puranic spirit',[9] rearranges and adapts the most popular story of the devi's killing of Mahisasura, which is part of the traditional subject matter of Sakta literature, within a Vaishnava framework as is clear from its stucture as a dialogue between the great sage, Shuka, and King Parikshit.

---

of Mayura, p. vii, NY: Columbia University Press, 1917). About the historical context, Krushna Charan Sahoo, the Odia compiler and editor of Sarala Das's *Chandi Purana*, which is the source text of this English translation, makes use of Mahisa's fight with Durga's troop of *dakinis* and *chandis* who are thrown all over the place, to allude to the destruction wreaked by Mughal invaders who went on a rampage destroying idols (p. 82). A similar observation is made by Kumkum Chatterjee: 'During the period of the Mughal conquest of Bengal, the imperial military machine was represented as a monster whom the Goddess Chandi, symbolizing Bengal's regional culture, had to vanquish', p. 1435; see 'Goddess Encounters: Mughals, Monsters and the Goddess in Bengal', in *Modern Asian Studies*, vol. 47, no. 5, Cambridge: Cambridge University Press, 2013: 1435–87.

[7] Such framing is a result of my reading of the essays in Alf Hiltebeitel and Kathleen M. Erndl (eds.), *Is the Goddess a Feminist?: The Politics of South Asian Goddesses* (New York: NYU Press, 2000).

[8] This approach was vaguely but strongly inspired by a reading of Erich Neumann's *The Great Mother: An Analysis of the Archetype*, trans. from German (Princeton, New Jersey: Princeton University Press, 1972).

[9] Coburn explains it as 'the spirit of multiformity and tolerance' (p. 346). Thomas B. Coburn, 'The Study of the Puranas and the Study of Religion', in *Religious Studies* vol. 16 no. 3, 1980: 341-52.

The rearrangement and adaptation have a divine sanction because it is the devi who instructs the poet during her nightly visitations. *ChP*, therefore, is *sruti* literature in which an old story makes a renewed appearance and will continue to appear in the imagination of any human conscious of existential challenges. Consequently, there may never be a retelling which is logically superior. Because of its stucture as a dialogue between Shuka and Parikshit, native scholars[10] of *ChP* have seen it mostly as derived from *Devi Bhagavata*, in which devi is seen as a manifestation of ultimate reality (Brahma). Perhaps rightly, because unlike the *Devi Mahatmya*[11] which mostly argues that all women embody qualities of devi, the *Devi Bhagavata* is more forthcoming about the complex nature of women as is in *ChP*. However, the metaphysical aspect of the devi, has often been used as a tool to propagate feminist ideologies of power and domination. But while the metaphysical aspect rarely helps the modern reader with material and worldly concerns to appreciate the relevance of a text as *ChP*, the feminist ideological position threatens to reduce the text to a

[10] My reference is only to Krushna Charan Sahoo, who has edited Sarala Das's *Chandi Purana*, which was published by Books and Books (Cuttack) in 1984. The English translation is of this text. My observation is also based on my reading of Cheever Mackenzie Brown's *The Triumph of the Goddess: The Canonical Models and Theological Visions of the Devi-Bhagavata Purana* (Albany: SUNY Press, 1990).

[11] For an extensive account of the contents of *Devi Mahatmya* and its sociological implications, I have referred Cynthia Humes's 'Is the Devi Mahatmya a Feminist Scripture?', in Alf Hiltebeitel and Kathleen M. Erndl (eds.), *Is the Goddess a Feminist?*, pp. 123–50. I began entering the text of *Chandi Purana* with the help of Thomas Coburn's *Devi Mahatmya: The Crystallization of a Goddess Tradition* (New Delhi: Motilal Banarsidass, 2002), and Cheever Mackenzie Brown's *The Triumph of the Goddess*. The *Devi Mahatmya* of *Markandeya Purana* is commonly believed to be the earliest account of Durga's slaying of the buffalo demon.

simplistic narrative about the superiority of the feminine, which, in turn, has given rise to debates about the gender of transcendent consciousness. Puranic texts on the devi represent femininity which is outside the ordinary and therefore, have transformed her into an object of awe and worship. However, it is the worldliness which resonates in the devi's manifestation as Chandi that makes *ChP* irresistible.

Sarala Das calls his composition variously as *Vishnu Purana*, *Sri Bhagavata* and *Chandi Purana*. The exordium gives the purpose of the narration which is embedded in the desire expressed by Parikshit, who was on the verge of death, having been bitten by the snake king Takshak, to hear *Vishnu Purana*. Chandi is a Vaishnavi who has been through many lives as Narmada Saraswati, the daughter of the creator Krupajal. As Saraswati, she was guilty of a minor offence and hence had to live in exile as the village Goddess Hingula at the holy site of Chandrabhaga in Oda rastra. Later, she shifted to Kanaka, Parshuramapatana, where she has been worshipped as Sarala Chandi for 1,32,000 years of Kali Yuga. It is she, Katyayani, who instructs the poet during her nightly visitations to write and thus Sarala Das's *ChP* acquires authority within a particular locale.

Whatever she dictates me during her nightly
Visitation, I write it down as soon as
The sun rises.

Through a quick genealogical account of the demonic clan and how the earth came to acquire demonic attributes, Shuka makes a deliberate arrival at the primaeval male desire for a woman. But it is the malevolent sexual desire of Kapilasingha that kick-starts the story. By a boon granted by Shiva, the demon king Kapilasingha had been empowered by 'enormous sexual desire to seduce women'. Frightened by his oppressive sexual behaviour, Kapilasingha's wife Dharmarekha escaped to Singhala where she took refuge as a buffalo in disguise. Yama's carrier, the buffalo Krtantaka was in Singhala and overpowered by desire, it chased Dharmarekha and ravished her. From their union was born a son with the body of a buffalo. In the meanwhile, Kapilasingha, who was searching for his wife, was led by a sage to Singhala. There, near Subarnagiri hills, he found his wife with the child. Dharmarekha seeks forgiveness for having lost her chastity but Kapilasingha, overcome with tenderness, takes her back and they settle down in a newly built city Jenabati, on the bank of Kamakshi. The son is named Mahisasura, the buffalo demon. Dharmarekha's faint resistance to her husband seems to have yielded a good result. In his love for his wife and child, Kapilasingha undergoes a transformation and they lead a happy family life.

Mahisasura grows up, trained in warfare and with an incorrigible desire for power and immortality. He undertakes 9,000 years of penance, forcing Brahma to grant him his wish to be 'the undisputed monarch of the three/Worlds' and that he 'won't be killed/In Narayana's hands. Vishnu's wheel/ Can't harm me; no man can put me to death.' Mahisasura was so utterly convinced of the powerlessness of the woman that he felt that he had finally achieved immortality. The asura then begins to acquire lordship over one dominion after another until all the kingdoms of Singhala come under his sway. He expanded his father's kingdom Jenabati and settled two lakh demons there. As a ferocious warlord, Mahisa first slays Tarakshi, the powerful king of Kurancheka, and then proceeds for a battle with Merusala, the fearsome king of Bajra, a kingdom at the foot of the Meru mountain. Mahisa tastes his first defeat at the hands of Merusala and is overcome with doubt and anxiety about the efficacy of Brahma's boon. He, however, gets ready for his next battle with Dhumraketu, who ruled the rich kingdom of Karancha. Dhumraketu's minister, however, tells the king that the latter's clan has historical affinity with the clan of Mahisasura after which the king sends his son Dhumralochana to welcome Mahisasura to their kingdom. Mahisasura, happy with the king's allegiance, ordains Dhumralochana as his charioteer. He next proceeds to Kusha, which was ruled by Prachandasura. Mahisa demands the services of Chanda and Munda, the powerful sons of the king of Kusha. Prachandasura rejects the demand, following which a fierce war ensues. The exploits of Chanda and Munda force Mahisasura to use his powers of invisibility but Chanda and Munda prove invincible. Mahisasura offers to make peace with Prachandasura and requests the services of Chanda and Munda whenever required. The king of Kusha accedes to his request and they make peace. Feeling smug after his territorial acquisitions, Mahisasura is seen riding with his army until he comes to Chandra island. The king Chandra Naumi, in the meantime, was arranging a *swayambara* for his beautiful daughter Chandrabati. For the wedding, he had invited 1,10,000 kings for his daughter to choose from. The poet names thirty-two kings and goes on to say that the sources of his subject are the *Bhagavata*, the *Vishnu Purana*, the Vedas and the eighteen Puranas.

I write it in my own ignorant way.
One lakh ten thousand kings have assembled
In Chandra island with lakhs of warriors
And attendants. To give an exhaustive list
Of all of them would be tiresome. My knowledge
Is no doubt limited. The *pandits* will not
Appreciate it. For the common men it will be
Dense. Therefore, I've quoted only some
Important names.

In the *swayambara*, the kings pitifully fail the test. Just then, Mahisasura descends upon the kingdom of Chandra and seeks to participate in the *swayambara*. Chandra Naumi rebukes him, saying he would not give his daughter to a *chandal*. Mahisasura is enraged and forcefully takes the test and passes it. The king then gives away his daughter to Mahisasura who requests that his two brothers-in-law Raktabirjya and Bidulaksha be allowed to accompany him in his triumphal march back to his kingdom. On their way back, Mahisasura invades the kingdom of Jambu and a bloody battle ensues. King Padmalabha of Jambu is eventually killed by Raktabirjya. Drunk with power, Mahisasura marches on and annexes the whole of Jambu island. But there was still Kulabati, which was a formidable kingdom on the southern coast of the sea ruled by two brothers Shumbha and Nishumbha. The brothers had Brahma's boon to rule the heavens and the earth but they would be burnt to ashes if they touched each other's head. The fierce battle with Shumbha and Nishumbha is led by Mahisasura's first line of command comprising Raktabirjya, Biraghanta, Chamara and Bemala. The second line of command is led by Jayasingha, Bajrasingha and Mahisasura. But Mahisasura loses the battle and surrenders to Shumbha who embraces him and offers him the kingdom of Kulabati as a sign of friendship. In his march for power, Mahisasura thus acquires both territories and more and more asura friends.

However, the heavens are yet to be conquered. A letter from Mahisasura, 'the monarch of all kingdoms', is issued to be carried by his messengers Sahasra and Prashasta to Indra:

Sri Mahisasura commands Indra of Amaravati
To present himself before him with Airavata,
Rambha, Parijata and Uchchaihsraba.

But Indra acts deplorably, killing the messengers. Andhaka, whose eyes had been plucked out by Mahisasura when he had advised the latter in his childhood to stop his wicked actions, had approached Shiva who had granted him the boon to see the past, present and future. He informs Shumbha and Nishumbha that the messengers had been killed by Indra. The two brothers set out for Amaravati, in a chariot pulled by a thousand lions. The timid Indra hardly puts up a fight and rushes to Brahma for help. Brahma says he has to take care of all beings and advises Indra to let Shumbha and Nishumbha rule Amaravati and asks him to stay with his *gandharvas* and apsaras in Brahma's abode. Meanwhile, the asura brothers continue to hold sway; they force Yama to flee in fear; and force Kubera to abandon his kingdom Alakapuri, and post their guards there. Having thus established their rule in the heavens, the brothers return with their booty to present to their lord Mahisasura in Jenabati.

It included
The jewels collected from the sea when, years ago,
The sea was being churned. Mahisa adorned
Himself with the robes and ornaments that Indra
Used to wear, and the rest, he gave away among
His commanders. Raktabirjya, Biraghanta
And Bidulaksha put the necklaces of the gods
Around their necks. All of Mahisa's followers
Revelled in drinking, dancing and playing musical
Instruments. At Mahisa's command, the charioteer
Decorated the chariot with nine kinds of gems
And yoked lions to it. As Mahisa adorned
The chariot, it flew into the sky at the speed
Of the wind. The gods, *gandharvas*, *dakshas*
And *kinnaras*, whoever were there in heaven fled
In fear. With his followers, Mahisasura entered
Amaravati, where he was received warmly.
Shumbha and Nishumbha offered him the coronation
Attire of Indra. They offered gems to Ratkabirjya,

Andhaka, Biraghanta, Kantimala, Chanda, Munda,
Bidulaksha, Bhaskar, Surabara, Bhagava,
Birabahu, Lohasura, Kanka, Dhanka, Kalanala,
Bahu, Subahu, Chanda, Prachanda, Umura,
Dumura, Sukha, Durmukha, Gila, Mahagila,
Tadaka and Bimukha. Praising Shumbha
And Nishumbha, Mahisa said, 'It's for you that
The entire heaven became ours'. He ordained
Kalaketu as the king of Sanjibanipura,
Biraghanta became the king of Hemabantapura;
The charge of Hiranyagarvapura was left
To Bidulaksha and Chamara and Bemala
Became the custodians of Alakapuri.

When in danger, the gods turn to Narayana and so they did.

Looking at Narayana's face,
All the gods wailed and wept. They were saying,
'You're our only Saviour. We have become
Slaves in our own homes. We have been robbed
Of our power and position.' A howl of grief
Filled the night air.

With great power, Mahisa lived in great fear. One day, which was the eighth day of the dark fortnight of Ashwin, Mahisa 'disguised as a buffalo was skulking at the foot of the Meru mountain' when he heard Narayana telling the gods how to kill Mahisa. 'In a mad fit he struck the mountain with his horns' which made the mountain crumble. The gods who dwelt therein were infuriated and it seemed 'as if the seven worlds were in flames'. Mahisa springs into action and makes elaborate plans to disempower the gods and invade Brahma's abode where the gods had taken refuge. Shumbha and Nishumbha protest, saying that all that he has achieved is because of Brahma and that he should give up his plans but Mahisa reacts in pain and anger.

'If he is our father, how does he think
Ill of us? A father unable to protect his family
Deserves to die.'

Parikshit became impatient to know what the gods did when the place was ablaze. Shuka starts his story of Sri Durga. Brahma fervently prays to the god of fire, from which emerges his sister 'sparkling like a gem'.

Her forehead was made of the fire of
Brahma; her face of that of Narayana;
Her teeth of Mahesvar's; eyes of God of Fire,
Nose of Indra; radiance of her face of Aditya;
Tongue of the Moon, cheeks of Yama; chest of
Kubera;

Armpit of God, the Formless; navel of Sanaka;
The folds on her abdomen of Ashwini Kumar;
The nose-rings of Yama and Brihaspati; thighs
Of Prajapati; feet of Ananta Basuki; toes of
The nine planets and Bhrigu; fingers of Kunda
Buds; the back of Hemabanta; the hair of the stars;
The belly of Baruna; the water in her body of Rain;
Her one thousand hands of forty-nine winds;
Her words of Yama and her holiness of
Vaishnavas.
She was as wise as Brahma; as enchanting
As Kamadeva; as warlike as Krishna; as learned
As Brihaspati; as boastful as Indra; as glorious
As the Moon; as radiant as the Sun; as cruel as
Yama;
As forbearing as the Earth; as swift as the Wind;
As sacred as the Meru; as charming as the Rain;
As solemn as Baruna, as captivating as Parvati
And as resolute as Kumara.
Listen, O King! She was born from the fire,
Contributed by each of the gods; her nature was
An amalgam of their attributes. Suddenly

The voice of Providence was heard from above:
She is the one who will save the world from
The powers of evil, so she is named Durga.

Brahma, on behalf of the gods, begs her to kill Mahisasura. Durga, who does not speak much, assures him and stretches out her hand to receive the gods' weapons, seemingly implying that unlike the gods, who constantly face the threat of usurpation and physical combat with their asura counterparts, and hence carry their own weapons, the Goddess is stepping into unconventional, though not unfamiliar, territory. However, Durga does not complain. She is powered from within by her natural tenacious resolve to protect and from without an animus embodied in the gods' weapons. At the same time, she is protected by her selfless purpose which is not only to preserve order but also to create conditions for regeneration. But her sparse speech seems to be an eloquent expression of her foresight about an impending upheaval.

Maheswari started her journey, riding a lion.
Her thousand hands with thousand weapons were
Outspread, her head touching the sky.
[...]
[...] The hem of her skirt hung over
Sixty-five *yojanas* of land when she moved along.
On a mountain to the north-east of a jungle
Called Uddana, on the banks of Saraswati,
She alighted and took her seat. At its foot was
Jenabati city, to its north was a banyan tree
Called Jata and to the far north was Kulabati city.
All those places were located near the Labana sea.
The gods in heaven were watching each of her
Movements carefully. Hiding her extra hands
Inside her body and her weapons in the *khechari*
Chariot, Katyayani stayed seated where she was.

Durga chooses to descend directly on a conflict zone in which the terms and conditions of the war have so far been laid down by Mahisa – aggression and cruelty, self-aggrandizement, and violence and disruption. It is difficult to ignore the poet's strategic use of the figures of the narrator and the narratee to imply the continuity in the tradition of war discourse. While the rules of Kurukshetra war did not permit a woman to participate in war in a deliberate act to suppress the warrior woman to manifest herself (the story of Amba and her desperate reappearance as Srikhandi in the *Mahabharata* is well known to be explained) as well as to project an idealized non-threatening image onto a woman, which we shall come to in the following paragraphs, *ChP* seems a deliberate counter to the fallacious cultural perception about the unnaturalness of women going to war. It is not to set new rules for women's participation in war or to encourage women to be war-like but to explain the conditions in which it may be natural for a woman to go to war and to alert the readers to the dangerous nature of such conditions.

Durga is noticed by Chanda and Munda who were having their midday bath in the river. It was unnatural for them to behold a beautiful young woman sitting all alone on a mountain. The brothers are met with a figure they are not used to and hence they ask:

[...] Where
Do you come from? Who is your husband?
Whose daughter are you? You're so young
And beautiful. What did you do that provoked
Your husband to forsake you? Are you
a demoness, a supernatural being, or a dweller
Of the forest?

Durga 'softly' rejects their projections of an ideal woman as one who can be identified as belonging to a man, be it a father or a husband and changes the frame of reference to explain her identity. At the same time, she deliberately narrates the fate of a woman who behaves in a way which can lead to disintegration of family and social life:

[...] O demons
Here are the answers to your queries
My mother is Fire and my father Anakara
As the daughter of Fire, I'm of Nirakara's clan.
My husband's name is God, the Almighty.
I'm ill-mannered and intolerant. I'm not loyal
To my husband as I'm not cut out for conjugal
Relationship. In the very first night, I refused
To sleep with him. In anger, he turned me
Out of the house. For my deviant behaviour
I failed to lead a family life and was forced
To come here for shelter.

She continues:

When I've given up
The hope of my life, should I fear the wicked
demons?

A confused Chanda[12] asks if she would want to be Mahisa's queen consort. 'Tell him that I have come here only for him', Durga replies. The two rush to their king and describe every

[12] Kala Trobe explains Durga as 'overwhelming and difficult to define'. 'Being the personification of all the power of good in the cosmos, Durga is overwhelming and difficult to define, exacerbating her quality of distance, particularly from the male or demonic of the species. However, she may be approached on a more personal level as mother of the universe, *Mataji*, in her kindly and pleasant aspect or, for women, as an exemplar of inner strength and overriding intelligence.' (*Invoke the Goddess: Visualisations of Hindu, Greek and Egyptian Deities*, Minnesota: Llewellyn Publications, 2000, p. 21).

part of her body in great detail which stirs Mahisa's lust. They return to her with Mahisa's gifts for her and implore:

O mother! The glory of a woman lies in having
A husband in her youth, and you are going to
achieve It.
The king has agreed to make you his wife.

Durga demands that Mahisa come to her. Mahisa is enraged and orders Chanda and Munda to bring her forcibly. Making it clear that she is not purposely seeking conflict, and seemingly trying to ward off prospects of physical aggression, Durga reminds them of ethical behaviour, that of a king towards his objects, and of a man towards a woman. The demons understand none of that and try to catch her. Durga lets out a 'roar of rage' and issues forth Chhaya (shadow Goddess) and Maya (the Goddess of illusion) blended as Kalaratri (the Goddess of death) who gulps down Chanda and Munda along with the other demons who were accompanying them. Mahisa, meanwhile, is sick with desire for Durga. Fearing that Chanda and Munda might have been killed, he asks Shumbha and Nishumbha to fetch her. Durga engages them in conversation and entices them with an offer of love, following which the demons let her in on the secret of their death. Now Durga wants them to dance. Anxious to please her, they dance and are cleverly led by Durga to touch each other's head. Forgetting Brahma's note of caution, the demons fall down dead. Mahisa sends all his commanders one after another and Durga, while firmly rooted in her conscious self, brings forth wild attributes from the dark depths of her being, variously embodied in sixty-four fierce goddesses, the *yoginis*. These *yoginis* lived on the flesh and blood of men and animals, and are hungry. Durga unleashes them on the demons who are annihilated and devoured by the *yoginis*. Each of Mahisa's commanders is seen begging for love and sex from the yoginis who use the opportunity to crush the demons to death. However, Raktabirjya, the demon of blood and semen, proves to be formidable. Durga had to issue forth one lakh *dakinis* to gulp every drop of blood that fell from Raktabirjya because numerous demons would be born from a single drop yet Raktabirjya seemed invincible. It is then that Durga shakes her sword from which appears Kalika who dwells in Narayani's (one of the *yoginis*) cutlass and 'devours the entrails of each demon killed by Narayani'. Raktabirjya is finally killed.

> [...] It was a ghastly sight to see someone
> Swallowing a demon, his head sticking out of
> Her mouth. Someone had swallowed the legs
> Of the demon while his hands were hanging from
> Her mouth. Another was gnawing at the ribs
> Of a demon. Someone had wrung a demon's neck
> And tucked him under her arm.

Terrified with the loss of his bravest commanders, Mahisa cowers and is overcome with self-doubt. Even more soldiers volunteer to fight on his behalf and are killed mercilessly. The time arrives for Durga to face Mahisa, who has started for the battlefield.

Just when Durga and her troops are revelling in the glory of their victory, the earth rises baying for blood as there are even more demons left to be killed. Durga invites numerous goddesses and orders them to seduce the demons and kill them. The *yoginis* and the earth feast on the corpses and the dance of death continues until Mahisa himself arrives near Ratnagiri mountain where Durga is stationed since the war began, and he uproots it with his buffalo horns. The mountain is uprooted and Durga loses her throne until she finds another seat on the Subarnachuda mountain. Mahisa's reaction alerts

Durga who realizes that she has to enter into physical combat with Mahisa. Both Mahisa and Durga transform themselves into lions and a fierce battle ensues. But Durga fails to kill Mahisa, who escapes to return with renewed vigour. Another battle follows and Mahisa escapes to hide in the sea. Durga is deeply worried and from within her issues forth another Goddess in white with four hands, four faces and red complexion. She reminds Durga that Mahisa will not die until he sees her naked form, according to a boon granted him by Brahma. Durga resists, saying that she will do no such thing and she couldn't care less if the earth is in peril.

Let not the wicked demon die; let the gods
Be driven away from heaven; let the nine
Islands of the world be destroyed. But I can't
Show my naked body to the three worlds.

While Mahisa is on the run, the Goddess persists, and Durga painfully understands the futility of her resistance.
'What a shame to expose
My nakedness to everyone!'

The Goddess reminds Durga of her commitment to preserve order and bring peace and Durga is forced to take the form of Chamunda, stripping herself naked. Mahisa who is lying down completely drained, stares into a deathly chaos as Chamunda steps on him and the buffalo demon breathes his last.

In his march to power, Mahisa had been defeated by the gods and *asuras* several times. Even after being granted the boon that no man would be able to kill him, he was aware of the decoys that Narayana would employ to kill him. Andhaka his minister had warned him that Narayana is known to take feminine forms. Desperate to claim agency in his inevitable death as the only way to hold power, Mahisa seems troubled by a sense of impotence in a world weighing against him and thus directs his frustration towards the feminine world. It becomes an absolute assault on feminine modesty when Brahma grants him his wish that he would die seeing a woman in her naked form. With Chamunda stepping on him, the asura, unlike Ravana or Kamsa, does not seem penitential but instead stares into the pathway to the womb, perhaps to be born again.

Durga's war with Mahisasura is an archetypal story about the terror of feminine power challenged by male brutality and malevolence. But the story also embodies a tragic threat to feminine modesty in a world seized by male lust and desire for domination. The earth's cry for blood and her desire to devour her own is a frightening expression of pain born of a realization that she is face to face with the most 'demonic of the species'[13] whom she has to destroy. Chamunda is an ideational manifestation become necessary because of the nature of challenge at hand. The moment of Durga's transformation is not a celebratory one of unbridled power but a distressing one because of the need for Durga's violent affirmation of redemptive love for her creation. Durga's naked form is unsightly and unbearable to the gods who flee the sight, while Shiva implores Durga, 'I pray to you to put your clothes on', to which Durga replies, 'Don't you know I have taken a vow not to cover my body?' Shiva becomes aware about her transformation as a catclysmic event which would change mankind's perception about a wondrous femininity forever.

URMISHREE BEDAMATTA

[13] Ibid.

1

Prayer to Sri Ganesh

Glory to Dadhibamana!
Glory to Bighnaraj, the Benevolent one!
He, who sees you for once,
Achieves his heart's desire.
He, whom you bless, wins fame and fortune.
Praise be to Girija's son, the Merciful,
Who broke one of his teeth in a scuffle with
Kartik, and who meditates in *khechari*
Posture. Slayer of demons, you copied down
The eighteen Puranas. *Yogi* of *yogis*,
You have conquered time, space
And repose. Your eyes look like the caves
Of the Meru mountain. You are often lost
In the joy of heavenly love. Your mission to
Protect the righteous and wipe out the wicked
Will continue as long as the moon
And the sun exist. Dressed in white,
You have the complexion
Of the blue water lily. You have no beginning,

Nor end. You manifest yourself in all
The elements that constitute the universe.
Vyasa sang the Puranas to you,
And you took them down. O Girija's son!
When, as a child, you were at play,
You held the sea in the palm of your hand,
Which, a moment later, disappeared into the air.
O my lotus-eyed Lord!
You instruct me what to write.
Girija's mercy enabled me to have your
Blessings which redeemed my fears.

Thus says Sarala Das, praying at the feet
Of Bighnaraj, the well-wisher of mankind.

2

Prayer to Goddess Sarala

In Satya Yuga, the Creator,
Known by the name of Krupajal, created
The whole universe. It was to him
That the great Goddess, a Vaishnavi
And the Saviour of the world, was born.
Narmada Saraswati was the name
Given to her, who, by her knowledge
In scriptures, pleased her father. Held guilty
Of a minor offence, her father cursed her.
She had to live in exile, by the name
Of Hingula, in Chandrabhaga, a holy
Place in Oda rastra in the Jambu island
Called Bharata. Later, she shifted to Kanaka
Parshuramapatana where she has been worshipped
As Sarala Chandi for one lakh and thirty-two
Thousand years of Kali Yuga. The Saviour
Of mankind and a great *yogini*, she is the one
Whom Sudramuni Sarala Das worships.

O Noble ones!
Pardon me for my mistakes. I have not done
Anything worthwhile in my life. I am ignorant,
Unlearned and unintelligent. I owe my debt
Of gratitude to Goddess Katyayani
Of Jankherpur who instructs me to write
The scripture. O Noble ones!
Whatever she dictates me during her nightly
Visitation, I write it down as soon as
The sun rises. I do as she says.
That I have become a Sudramuni
Is because she wants me to be so.

3

Mahisasura's Meditation

Cursed for his childish prank,
Parikshit, the king of Kuru dynasty,
Was bitten by Takshak on the left side
Of his nose. The painful effect of poison
Made every nerve in his body tense.
In bitter agony, he prayed to Narayana
To save him from the pangs of death.
It was then that Shuka,
A great sage, well versed in the Vedas
And Puranas, met him.

The king bowed to him in respect,
Offering him finery, earrings and gems.
Most politely, he begged him, 'Glory to you,
O sage! I implore you to fulfil my wishes.
See, I've no son; my clan is on the verge
Of extinction, and I'm at death's door,
Being bitten by Takshak.' With consolatory
Words, the sage said, 'Listen to the *Vishnu Purana*

Attentively; you'll be blessed with a son
And conveyed to Vishnu's abode after death.
Now perform the rites required for listening
To the scripture.' When it was done, Parikshit
Said, 'O sage! Narayana incarnated himself
Hundreds and thousands of times to wipe out
The demons. Of these, his incarnation as Durga,
Who slew Mahisasura in war, amazes me most.
Tell me the story of Chandi and put
My anxiety to rest.' Sage Shuka began:

'Simhika of Kashyap's clan gave birth
To a son named Rahu, whose son was
Jambu, grandson, Japasura and great-grandson,
Khajara. Khajara had a son, Angira by name.
Angira's son was called Amaya and grandson,
Lohasura. Lohasura's son was Andhaka
And Andhaka's son was Tadaka. Tadaka had
A son named Maya, whose son was Bajrabahu,
Grandson, Maruchi and great-grandson, Kalinchi.
In Satya Yuga, while Narayana was asleep
In Saraswati's lap, Tadaka went on destroying
The holy places and tormenting the sages. At that
Time Shiva burnt Kama to ashes, and his son,
Kumar slew Tadaka. Tadaka's son mounted
An attack on heaven, forcing Indra to flee.'
Surprised, Parikshit prayed to the sage to speak
More about it. Shuka continued:

'In an unexpected situation, Rahu was put
To death; the body of the demon with a thousand
Hands was cut in half. Listen, O Parikshit!

In Satya Yuga, the three worlds were submerged
By the deluge. While having a yogic slumber
In Saraswati's lap, Narayana blew his nose,
From which two demons, Madhu and Kaitabha
Were born. He stationed them in heaven where
They grew up. They could walk on water without
Getting their feet wet. Enamoured of Saraswati's
Beauty, they made amorous advances to her.
Annoyed, she roused Narayana from sleep
And complained to him against them.

His eyes glinting angrily, Narayana stood up
With the wheel in his hand. Scared, the demons
Begged, "O Lord! We have committed
A grievous crime in our ignorance. We must
Pay for it. We pray to you to kill us at a place
Where there will be no water." They knelt down
Exposing their thighs. Narayana held them
By their arms and crushed them with his mace
Until they turned to a pulp. He hurled their
Flesh at the water, which became known as
The earth. As the earth was made from
The demons' flesh, it contained all their
Attributes in it. The first king to rule
The earth was Mahidas, by name.'

To dispel the doubts that had clouded his mind,
Parikshit begged the sage for more details,
To which the sage replied:

'Listen, O King! Saudas, Mahidas's son,
Had a disciple named Jalataranga. His son,

Medha and grandson, Krutakeshi were hostile
To the gods and the sages. Krutakeshi's son,
Trijatasura drove away the gods from heaven.
His son was Bhaskar, grandson, Bajrasingha
And great-grandson, Kapilasingha. Mahisasura
Was born to Kapilasingha.

After twenty-four years of Kapilasingha's
Unflinching devotion to Lord Shiva, the Lord
Was pleased to offer him a boon. Kapilasingha
Begged him for empowering him with
Enormous sexual vigour to seduce women
And overpower them in the act of sex.
Receiving the boon, he went on ravishing
Women, one after another.
Frightened by his aggressive sexual behaviour,
His wife, Dharmarekha, left him and sheltered
In Singhala island in the guise of a buffalo.
After combing many islands and not finding
Her, Kapilasingha returned home with
A heavy heart.

Krutantaka, the buffalo, who was Yama's
Carrier, used to stay in Singhala. It was a
Sunday, the new moon day of the month
Of Bhadrab on which Krutantaka caught
Sight of the cow buffalo. Tempted to have her
At any cost, he followed her excitedly. Seeing him,
She began to run, Krutantaka chasing her
All the way, at a speed more than that of the wind.
After running for a distance of nine lakh
Yojanas, she stopped under a *sinsapa* tree

In the Subarnagiri hills on the bank of river
Kamakshi that flowed through a jungle. It was
There that Krutantaka pounced on her and had
Sex with her most aggressively.
It resulted in the birth of a son,
With the body of a buffalo that looked
As bright as gold and as radiant as fire.

While looking for his wife in a jungle,
Kapilasingha met Sage Kapila and made friends
With him. Learning from him about his missing
Wife, the sage said to him,
"No woman can take the place of a wife.
The absence of a wife bears heavily on a man.
Once, while I was in Singhala, I saw a pair
Of buffaloes engaged in sex. The cow buffalo
Was pleading, 'I am not an animal like you.
I'm Kapilasingha's wife, Dharmarekha.
You're God's carrier; I'm a demoness It is
Not proper on your part to touch me.' Paying
No heed to her appeal, he had sex with her."
So saying, the sage disappeared. Kapilasingha,
Brimming with hope, left for Singhala island.

Reaching the Subarnagiri hills, he met
His wife who was sitting there with a child.
Delighted by the sight of the child,
Kapilasingha forgot all about his craze for sex
And women. Embarrassed, Dharmarekha
Returned to her human form and told him,
"Failing to bear with your sex urge, I forsook
You and came here. Krutantaka, Yama's carrier,

Raped me. I've demeaned myself, losing my
Chastity. Don't think of me any longer. I'm
A disgrace to the demon community. Better
Leave me to my fate." Kapilasingha told her
Soothingly, "I won't leave you alone. We'll live
Together here with our son." He built a city
On the bank of Kamakshi and named it Jenabati.
He named his son Mahisasura.

Mahisasura grew up and learnt the skills
Of war. Then, he went into meditation for
Nine thousand years, living only on water.
Thinking on Brahma, he raised
A sacrificial fire, and cutting pieces of flesh
From his body, consigned to it. In spite of
So much austerity, Brahma was not to be seen.
He continued his meditation for another twenty-one
Thousand years. At last he entered the pit of fire,
Caring least for his life. Surprisingly,
His body did not burn. It took a total of eighty
Thousand years to attract Brahma's attention.
Mahisa's steadfast devotion panicked the gods.
Rudra, the Moon, Yama, the Wind, Brihaspati,
Indra, the Sun, Baruna and Kubera proceeded
To Yashobantipur to inform Brahma about it.
Their palms against their cheeks, they briefed
Brahma the reason for their concern.

Brihaspati said, "O Creator of the universe,
Cause of causes, Ocean of Kindness!
You're Maker of the new world.
You created fifty-six crores of living beings;

You've no beginning. You've attained *siddhi*;
Your mind is pure, you've protected your
Creation from the fury of the deluge. When
You're awake, creation goes on; when you're
Asleep, the deluge takes place. We've no words
To describe your glory."'

Thus says Sarala Das, praying at the feet
Of Brahma, the greatest of all gods
And the Redeemer of all souls.

x x x

Sage Shuka continued:
'Listen, O Parikshit!
Finding the gods in dismay, Brahma asked,
"O Gods! Why are you fretting?"
Brihaspati replied, "Demon Mahisasura
Of Rahu's clan has been in meditation
In Singhala island, praying to you to become
Immortal." Indra feared, "He will occupy
Heaven." Kubera said, "He'll oust me from
My position." Yama added, "He'll dethrone me."
Brihaspati complained, "His success will cause
Consternation among the gods."

Realizing that it was a difficult situation,
Brahma replied, "I'll visit him now. I'll bless
Him with a boon, commensurate with his devotion.
In the meantime, all of you take necessary steps
To protect your wealth and position. Let me
Know from him what he likes to have before
I do anything. Now go to your abode without

Any apprehension. Know that your safety
Is my responsibility." So saying, he sat
On the swan, his carrier, and started his journey,
Followed by *brahmarsis*, such as Basistha,
Vishwamitra, Bamadeva, Agasti, Paulasti,
Satamanu, Valmiki, Narada, Bibhandaka,
Markanda, Sudeva, Varadwadasha, Sumanta,
Rishyashringa, Kaushika and Bhrigu,
Three crores of *dakshas* and disciples.
They went past the seven worlds and reached
Singhala island. They found Mahisa's hermitage
Under the *sinsapa* tree on the Subarnagiri
Hills on the banks of Kamakshi. All were surprised
By Mahisa's devotion, the like of which they
Had never seen nor heard before. The sages
Settled themselves on the summit of the hills.
Alighting from the swan, Brahma proceeded
To the sacrificial fire, but found no one there.
When he put out the fire by sprinkling some water
From his *kamandalu*, he caught sight of a red,
Radiant object inside the pit. It was Mahisa.
He had no nails, nose, nor legs; he looked like
A pillar made of gem. Taking some nectar
In his right hand, he sprinkled it over
His body. And lo! With the touch of nectar,
His limbs began to grow and his former self
Restored. He was of red complexion with
The head of a buffalo that touched the sky.
When Brahma offered him a boon, he flew
Into a rage and bawled at him, "What an ordeal
I had to pass through all these years! Who are you?
Where have you come from? Why did you disturb

My meditation? What a boastful brahmin
You are! I must take your life today." Brahma
Replied calmly, "I'm Brahma". Mahisa cried out,
"I don't believe it unless you show me
The proof. You could have spoken to me through
A voice from above! I won't trust you unless
You show me the signs of Brahman." Brahma
Showed him his real form with four heads:
The left one was the face of a guru, the right one
Of the Creator, the one on the front was of Brahma
And the rear one of Biranchi. He had eight
Hands, carrying bow, arrow, mace, staff,
Kamandalu, rosary and the Vedas. He had
Twelve holy signs on his body. He was reading
Out the Vedas rhythmically that vibrated through
The air. He was wearing a cloth, the front end
Of which was tucked to his waist at the back.
He had long hair and sandalwood marks
On his forehead. He was in a yogic posture.
O Parikshit! How can I describe him who is
The Creator of the universe? The demon saw
His huge form that had pervaded the three worlds.
He was blessing him by stretching one of his
Hands and saying, "Now tell me what you
Wish to have".

Making an appeal to the Almighty, Yama,
The Wind, the Fire, the Water and the Sky
To be witnesses, Mahisa said, "If you're so
Kind, bless me that I'll outlive the four Ages,
Until the time of the next deluge. Yama can't
Claim me; no disease can weaken me.

My body will be as strong as thunder;
No arrow nor weapons can pierce into it,
Even it can withstand the weight
Of a mountain. Fire can't burn me;
Water can't drown me, the curse of sages
Can't harm me. I'll attain *siddhi* in *yoga*
And none in the three worlds can conquer me.
Indra, Rudra, Baruna, Yama and the Sun will sing
My glory. With the help of *uluka vidya*,
I'll be able to disappear or take any form as
And when I wish. The gods will flee their
Abode in fear; the Wind and the Fire won't dare
Ravage my kingdom. Space and Time can't
Bind me. I'll master all the sixty-four skills
Of *yoga*. I'll have the power to see the unseen.
I'll be the undisputed monarch of the three
Worlds. The sages and brahmins will serve
At my feet. No one in the three worlds, including
Brahma, Vishnu and Maheswar can challenge
Me in war. As long as the moon and the sun
Exist, nothing can stop me from doing what
I want. The fear of Krishna induced me
To invoke you. Bless me that I won't be killed
In Narayana's hands. Vishnu's wheel
Can't harm me; no man can put me to death."

"So be it!" Brahma blessed him,
"You'll enjoy all your powers as long as I exist."

The sun had set by the time Brahma
Left for his abode. Empowered by Brahma's
Boon, Mahisa embellished Jenabati,

The city ruled by him, which exceeded
The beauty of Baraswatipur. All the demon kings,
Hearing about Mahisa receiving a rare boon,
Submitted themselves to him.'

4

Mahisasura's Conquest of Kurancheka

'Soon the demon kings, one after another,
Pledged their allegiance to Mahisasura.
They included Kantimala, the son of Maya,
Chamara and Bemala, sons of Bajranga
Of the kingdom of Bilanka, Hiranaksha
Of Madhurya kingdom, Dhumralochana
Of Mukhayeka and King Chandra of Ajan.
All the kingdoms of Singhala island came under
His sway. Extending the territory of Jenabati
To four lakh *yojanas*, he settled two lakh
Demons there.

On the road to monarchy, he moved
His troops to Kurancheka, a kingdom ruled by
A powerful king, Tarakshi, to invade it.
Occupying nine *yojanas* of land on the north
Bank of river Swadhabi, they camped there.
When the whole kingdom resonated with

The din and noise of the soldiers, the messengers
Informed Tarakshi, "Mahisasura has arrived
In our land to attack us. He is invincible. He has
Brahma's boon. The kings of Singhala
Island, after being forced to concede defeat,
Are now serving at his feet." Enraged, Tarakshi
Commanded his army to get ready for the battle.

Riding tigers, the king and his five crore
Warriors marched on until they met the enemy.
Tarakshi was startled to see Mahisa's huge army,
As large as the sea. Soon after the battle started,
Tarakshi's troops were overpowered. Kantimala
Went on slaughtering them like a wild elephant
In a garden of banana trees. It perplexed
Tarakshi to see the number of his soldiers reduced
To one lakh only, and all their tigers captured.
With the surviving soldiers, Tarakshi knifed into
Mahisa's army and battled hard to protect
His kingdom. Kantimala, raising a war cry,
Hit the enemy lethally; four of his soldiers
Could kill Tarakshi's one lakh soldiers. Impatient
And furious, Tarakshi launched a counter-attack
Targeting Kantimala, knocking him flat on
The ground, unconscious. Seeing their commander
Lying senseless, the soldiers decided to make
A hasty retreat. But, the situation took a turn
When Chamara and Bemala reached
There in a chariot. They showered arrows on
Tarakshi, which broke into pieces,
Unable to pierce into the king's body. When all their
Attempts to subdue Tarakshi failed, they fetched

The *brahmasara* from Mahisa's hand and shot
At him. It hit him on the head, and, like a tree,
He fell down on the ground, dead. Chamara
And Bemala chopped his head with a battle-axe
And hurled it into the sea.

Mahisa's soldiers plundered all the wealth
And riches of Kurancheka and carried them
Away to Singhala. Mahisa's kingdom was now
Extended to eleven *yojanas*. Death feared
To enter the kingdom. The Sun and the Wind
Dared not show their rage there. As days
Passed, Mahisasura's fame and fortune
Rose phenomenally.'

5

Mahisasura's Battle with Merusula

'On a Sunday, the eighth day of the bright
Fortnight of the month of Ashwin, Mahisasura
Invaded the kingdom of Bajra, situated at
The foot of the Meru mountain and ruled by
King Merusula. A battle broke out between
Mahisasura and Merusula that continued
For one hundred days. Both the armies
Suffered heavy casualties; the battlefield
Was soaked with blood, and the earth
Rocked violently. Causing panic among
The enemy, Kantimala, Chamara and Bemala
Fought so valiantly that the eyebrows of the gods
Were raised. Putting up a brave fight,
Merusula killed many of Mahisa's soldiers
With his mace. Unable to face Merusula,
The soldiers began to retreat when Kantimala

Intervened. With words of inspiration
He ordered his soldiers to fight bravely.

Listen, O Parikshit!
For his unflinching devotion to Hemavanta,
Merusula was blessed with immortality.
While in war, Rudhipa and Lochana,
The commanders of a king of Singhala
Attacked Merusula with all their might.
Flying into a fury, Merusula hit Lochana's
Head with his mace that made him fall
To the ground, unconscious. With a second
Blow he left him completely immobile.
Next, he charged at Rudhipa with a spade
And vanquished him. Seeing Kantimala
Left alone, Chamara and Bemala rushed
To him to provide help, but they were
Soon overpowered by Merusula's soldiers
Who surrounded them and countered
Each of their attacks.

Considering that he was in a difficult situation,
Mahisa joined the battle himself. It became
Sunset; the battle ended inconclusively.
Realizing that Merusula was as invincible
As he was, Mahisa left for Singhala in dismay.
A doubt cropped up in his mind: Was Brahma's
Boon true or false?'

6

Dhumralochana Ordained as a Charioteer

'O King Parikshit!
On a Thursday, the fourth day of the dark
Fortnight of Chaitra, Mahisasura resumed
His journey to conquer more kingdoms.
On the way, he came across a kingdom called
Karancha that impressed him most. Each
House there had a golden urn and flags
Atop it. With a large army at his command,
He camped there, deciding to invade it.
Udesh, the minister, informed King Dhumraketu
About Mahisa's arrival in their land. When
The king wanted to know what brought him
There, the minister said, "He and you belong
To the same clan. There was a king called
Kalpasura, who, cursed by Basistha,
Turned to a demon. He had a son named
Manudaksha. His sons were Raksha and Vaksha.
Raksha had two sons, Heti and Praheti.

Who had three sons: Mali, Sumali and
Malyabanta. Malyabanta's son was named
Madana Mahadeva and grandson, Matanga
Sadashiba. Malyabanta, who used to stay
In Lanka, came back to Karancha island
For fear of Vishnu. Matanga's son was
Bilochana and grandson, Hiranya. Hiranya
Had a son called Bailochana and grandson,
Bali. Bali's son was Madalochana
And his son, Kalabimochana. You're
His son and your son is Dhumralochana."
Glad to hear it, the king sent for his son,
Asking him to welcome Mahisasura
With plenty of gifts. On the seashore
Of Karancha island, Dhumralochana met
Mahisa with the presents. Introducing
Dhumralochana to him, Kantimala
Said, "He offers these presents as
A gesture of goodwill. The king of the island
Owes his allegiance to you." Most humbly,
Dhumralochana invited Mahisa to the palace
Where he was given a hearty welcome,
Followed by celebrations all over the kingdom.
Greatly entertained with their hospitality,
Mahisa spent five days there. He ordained
Dhumralochana as his charioteer and returned
To Singhala jubilantly.'

7

Mahisasura Concedes Defeat to Chanda and Munda

'In a bid to expand his territory beyond
Singhala island, Mahisasura set out with
A large army in quest of new dominions. It was
A Monday of the bright fortnight of Kartik.
The sound of gongs and trumpets
Filled the air. As the soldiers marched on,
A cloud of dust rose, hiding the sun from
View. There were eighty *kharbas* of warriors
And seven *padmas* of attendants, each warrior
Riding a tiger and equipped with weapons,
Such as lance, sword, bow, arrow, mace
And spear. Heaven resonated with their war
Cry, which was as deafening as the roar
Of the sea. On the full moon day of Kartik
They left Singhala, and passing through Karancha,
Reached Kusha island.

Known for his piety, Prachandasura,
The king of Kusha island, lived the life of a *yogi*,
His body smeared with ash, long matted hair
Hanging from his head. He was in ochre clothes,
The sacred thread running from the shoulder
To the waist, a *dambaru* in one hand and a trident
In the other. Death dared not visit his land ever.
He commanded an army of fourteen crore soldiers,
All of whom led the lives of *yogis*. His kingdom,
Measuring forty lakh *yojanas*, was inhabited
By people of eighteen castes, each one steadfastly
Loyal to the king. With Lord Shiva's blessing on him
He ruled his kingdom without the fear of rivalry.

When the sound of gongs and trumpets
Was heard from a distance, the messengers
Came running to him to inform, "O Lord!
Mahisasura has sneaked into your kingdom.
Because of Brahma's boon, he has been mightier
Than before. You're Narayana yourself;
The three worlds know you have been living since
Satya Yuga. You're competent enough to decide
Whether you want peace or war. You have been
In Lord Shiva's good graces from time immemorial.
He has received Brahma's boon only recently."

Hearing that Mahisasura was camping under
The banyan tree on Karunakar mountain, on
The banks of river Narmada, Shivapada,
The minister, told the king, "May I meet Mahisasura
And ask him the purpose of his visit? We'll try
To be friendly with him; if he doesn't reciprocate,

Battle is the only option." When the king consented,
He met Mahisasura with precious gifts.
He found him with Chamara and Bemala
And surrounded by warriors decked in gems
And looking like heavenly beings. Pleased to see
The gifts, Chamara and Bemala presented him
Before the king and said, "The minister of King

x x x

Prachandasura has come to greet you. A devotee
Of Vishnu, he has been a minister since Satya Yuga."
Offering the gifts, which seemed to please Mahisasura,
The minister said humbly, "O Lord! My king
Has conveyed his love to you. He is Shiva's son
And you're Brahma's son. This forges a bond
Between you two." Mahisasura replied, "Listen,
O minister! Let your king know that Kantimala,
The king of Singhala has surrendered to me with
His wealth and riches. The king of Karancha island
Submitted to my authority with his army. Your
king, Prachandasura, has two sons, Chanda
And Munda. If he is genuinely interested in
Making friends with me, let him surrender
His sons to me. It'll strengthen our friendship
For years to come. If he disagrees, he'll have
To face my wrath. I'll kill him and eat his flesh.
I'll reduce his kingdom to rubble." He bit his lips
In anger and stood up like a column of fire
That touched the sky.

Returning, Shivapada informed the king,
"O King! Empowered by Brahma's boon,

Mahisasura is on his way to conquer all
The islands. His oppression has been too much for
The earth to bear. He was born not to a man,
But to a buffalo. He agrees to your proposal
Of peace on the condition that you surrender
Your sons to him. He'll make them his commanders
And conquer the world utilizing their services."
Breaking down in grief, Prachandasura muttered,
"How can I part with my sons? I may give away
My army and my wealth. I may carry out his
Instructions, but how can I live without my sons?"
Saying so, he burst into tears. Collecting himself,
He commanded his minister to get the troops
Ready for the battle.

Blowing trumpets and bugles, Prachandasura's
Soldiers, their bodies smeared with ashes,
Marched on, with *dambaru* in one hand and trident
In the other. The sound of fourteen crores of *dambarus*
Blown at a time deafened the three worlds. Riding bulls,
The warriors marched ahead, raising a war cry
To repel the invading forces, which had spread
Like a sea. Both the armies met each other
On the banks of the river. Chanda and Munda,
Seated on tigers, assured their father,
"Don't worry as long as we are here". The king
Replied, "Listen! Mahisasura is hell-bent on
Capturing both of you. So, take care and position
Yourselves in the rear." Seeing Prachandasura's
Troops, Kantimala told Mahisasura, "Prachandasura
Has come with his army to battle against us.
It is because you asked for his sons." Mahisa

Commanded Bemala and Kantimala, "Move
Quickly and prevent Prachandasura from
Advancing further. In the meantime, using
The *mantra* given to me by Brahma, I'll disappear
Into the sky, from where I'll locate Chanda
And Munda and capture them. If I fail,
I'll consider Brahma's boon is of no use."

Mahisa flew into the sky, making himself invisible.
Seeing Chanda and Munda playing in the waters
Of Ganga, he alighted there like a bird. By that time,
His soldiers had already gathered there. Seeing
The enemy in front of them, Chanda and Munda
Rose from the waters, waving maces, and charged
At them. Finding the battle gaining momentum,
Mahisa shouted at Chanda and Munda,
"Wait! Wait! How could you master the skills
Of war at so tender an age?" Turning to his soldiers,
He instructed, "I'm amazed by their outstanding
Performance. Don't kill them. We'll catch them
Alive and take them away with us." At this,
The soldiers surrounded Chanda and Munda
Enraged, the heroes of Kusha island went on
The offensive, which caused havoc among
The enemy. In a short time, Mahisa's two thousand
Soldiers were eliminated; the rest stood as dumb
As a tribe of goats. The two brothers made
A formidable combination; the sight of blood
Doubly excited them. Boiling mad, Mahisasura
Commanded the panicked soldiers to fight back.
They rained down arrows on them, but by
The grace of Lord Shiva, their bodies had turned

To thunder, strong enough to withstand the attack.
Furious, Chanda and Munda retaliated
Destroying one lakh soldiers, reducing
The strength of Mahisa's army to three hundred.
Awestruck, Mahisa watched Chanda and Munda
Chasing those who were on the run.
Mahisa disappeared into the sky where he met
Kantimala, Chamara and Bemala. He told
Them, "It's better to draw a treaty of peace
Than to fight a losing battle. Let's meet
King Prachandasura and make friends with
Him. If he declines to accept our offer, we'll
Resume the battle with renewed energy."
Unarmed and barefooted,
They went to meet the king.

Shivapada informed the king, "Leaving the battle
Midway, Mahisasura has come here to make peace
With us. If we don't oblige him, we'll incur God's
Displeasure." As Mahisasura arrived, Shibapada
Bowed at his feet and told him, "Both the kings
Are now friends to each other. The history of your
Family reveals that both of you have the same
Lineage, you being the king's grandson."
Pleased with their hospitality, Mahisa spent four
To five days there. When it was time for him
To leave, he requested the king to help him in times
Of need and that he would like to have his sons
With him. Prachandasura offered him five
Of his commanders, thousands of soldiers
And his sons. Reaching Singhala, Mahisa held
A ceremony in honour of Chanda and Munda.

He ordained them the rulers of Jenabati,
A city with a population of four lakh demons.'

Glory to you, O God, the Merciful,
The lotus-eyed one! Let my devotion to you
Be single-minded. O Friend of the poor
And Protector of the righteous!
I'm Sarala Das, son of Sarala Chandi,
Kripajal's daughter. Too feeble and too
Ignorant as I am, I write as the Goddess
Instructs me. Her eyes are like the lotuses
And face like the moon. O my Saviour!
I pray at your feet.

8

Mahisasura's Marriage with Chandrabati

With greatest respect, King Parikshit
Asked Shuka, 'What did Mahisasura do after
He occupied the three islands: Singhala, Karancha
And Kusha? Tell me about his heroic exploits;
That'll wash away the sins of my previous births.'
Sage Shuka, proficient in scriptures, began:

'In an auspicious moment
On a Thursday, the eleventh day
Of the bright fortnight of the month of Magha,
Mahisa led along
His troops southwards, among the sounds
Of trumpets and bugles. The soldiers followed
Him from behind; Chamara and Bemala led
From the front; Kantimala was at his right,
Flanked by Chanda and Munda. As they
Goose-stepped, the earth rocked under their
Weight, while the gods in heaven watched them

In silence; some of them fleeing in panic.
Leaving Singhala, they reached Karancha, crossing
The Labana sea of twenty-six *yojanas*. Karancha
Measured forty *yojanas*. From there, they went
To Kusha island, crossing the Nila Sea of
Thirty lakh *yojanas*. Seeing Chanda and Munda
Enjoying Mahisa's favour, Prachandasura
And Shibapada were extremely happy. Then,
They ventured into the Chandra sea, eating
Whatever came their way, before reaching
Chandra island. They started ransacking it
As soon as they got there.

Chandra Naumi, the king of the island that
Measured thirty *yojanas*, belonged to the clan
Of Bhusanda Kaka. He lived with his wife,
Chandrarekha and daughter, Chandrabati,
Who was a paragon of beauty. Unable to find
A suitable groom for her, the king held
A *swayambara*, to which five lakh kings
From far and wide were invited. There was
A mountain there, Chandragiri by name,
In which the king had stored seven casks
Of nectar. It was guarded by five crore *gandharvas*.
It was from that mountain that the Moon,
The ruler of the Chandra sea, used to rise,
Lighting the whole island. The sea surrounding
Padma island was ruled by Bedabrahma. The sea
Encircling Ananta island in the north-east was
Under the authority of Aditya, from where the sun
Used to rise. Dhurjati was the king of the sea
Surrounding Kusha island. Kubera was the king

Of the sea around Kurancheka island.
The sea surrounding Kusha island was
Under the sway of Yama. Mahisasura
Stopped at the foot of the Chandragiri mountain,
Ransacking the adjacent areas.'

Parikshit begged the sage to tell him about
Chandrabati's *swayambara*. Sage Shuka said:

'King Chandra Naumi ordained one lakh
Ten thousand kings as prospective grooms for
His daughter. They were: Aranyaka of Kamoda,
Kalabali of Chandapur, Kanti of Matangapur,
Chandraksha of Akshana, Animisa of Ananga,
Niranjan of Niranjan, Nirmalasen of Kalinga,
Ichhapadma of Palasha, Juganta of Ajamatra,
Aindra of Sarada, Jalataranga of Jalandhar,
Prabalasingha of Naudha, Krutasen of Sudarsan,
Ridhipati of Matanga, Harisen Rai of Parardha,
Aswamali of Burdwan, Bhagasen of Atuta,
Satasingha of Srikhandi, Runakeshi of Matanga,
Basantadeva of Kashyapa, Padmasen of Adita,
Sikharasen of Murdula, Karnamali of Satpadma,
Sarajati of Madhurya, Biranchi of Madhuban,
Madhuindu of Talam, Kikaliswar of Kikali,
Mala of Marbati, Sarasi of Chakrabratika,
Hiranyakachapa of Biraja, Kalingasen of Samidha,
Krutantika of Dehuka and many others. As told
By their father, Raktabirjya and Bidulaksha
Offered the guests golden thrones to sit
And entertained them with best hospitality.'

O mother Katyayani! O moon-faced One!
I owe my debt of gratitude to you for
Stimulating me to write. The sources of my
Subject are the *Bhagavata Vishnu Purana*,
The *Vedas* and the eighteen *Puranas*.
I write it in my own ignorant way.
One lakh ten thousand kings have assembled
In Chandra island with lakhs of warriors
And attendants. To give an exhaustive list
Of all of them would be tiresome. My knowledge
Is no doubt limited. The *pandits* will not
Appreciate it. For the common men it will be
Dense. Therefore, I've quoted only some
Important names. Sitting in Jambu island,
I'm talking about Kusha island, as told by Vyasa.

x x x

Sage Shuka told Parikshit:
'The kings attending the *swayambara* were
Entertained by the king and his sons, Raktabirjya
And Bidulaksha. The river Chandrabhaga,
Originating from Vishnu's feet, flowed there.
Cursed by Prajapati, the moon began to wane
After the full moon day; its size reduced each day,
Until it became a crescent. Feeling guilty and full
Of remorse, it plunged into the river. But,
Instead of dying out, it began to wax day by day
Till it reached its full form. Since then,
Chandrabhaga had been held as a sacred river.

The *swayambara*, held on the banks
Of the river, started with King Chandra

Addressing the invitees: "O kings!
Lend me your ears. I've taken a vow
Since the day I happened to witness
The *swayambara* of King Nairuta's daughter,
Shakuntala, in Jambu island. It was a Sunday,
The third day of the bright fortnight
Of the month of Magha. While travelling
In the air in my chariot when I heard a loud
Noise. Looking below, I saw a boisterous crowd
Assembled at a place in Jambu island. Alighting
From the chariot, I learnt that a *swayambara*
For the king's daughter was going on. The guests
Were surprised to see me, but my presence delighted
Shakuntala the most, who came forward and put
A gem necklace around my neck. I brought her
With me and married her here. She gave birth to
A daughter, named Chandrabati. Unable to find
A suitable groom for her, I've arranged
A *swayambara* and invited all of you. My
Daughter, Chandrabati, is a paragon of beauty;
None in the three worlds can match her. The moon
Has built a monument, studded with eight kinds
Of gems, to the north-east of the island. Its base
Measures twenty-five *yojanas* and height one lakh
Yojanas, with Baruna sitting on the top of it.
The gems on it lighted the whole island.
All you've to do is to shoot an arrow
Which must get in through it.
One who wins the competition
Will marry my daughter.
This *swayambara* will continue for seven days,
Allowing everybody a chance to win."

Hearing this, all the kings flocked to the monument,
Riding their respective carriers. Soon the place
Became crowded and noisy. The monument
Scared everyone. King Sudirgha said,
"There can be no one on the earth to do it,
Except Jamadagni's son, Parshurama." The kings
Looked at each other in despair; the task seemed
Too difficult for them to accomplish. They asked
Chandra Naumi to show his daughter to them;
That might inspire them to meet the challenge.
The king asked Raktabirjya to fetch her there.

Chandrabati, decked in finery, arrived
Ceremonially, among the sounds of music
And ululation. Seeing her, the kings exclaimed,
"What a beauty! None in the three worlds
Except Parvati, can equal her. The shine of her face
Will make the moon look paler, and the glow
Of her body will make the gems fade into
Insignificance. We are no match for her;
If she is the moon, we are the stars.
We'll never forget this embarrassing
Experience in our lives." King Chandramauli
Of Chanchal kingdom interrupted, 'O kings!
One who passes the test will marry the princess,
No matter, whether he is handsome or ugly.
What have you got to do with her beauty? Come,
Let's see, who can do it." At this, the kings got up,
Ready to try their luck. Karnakeshi, the king
Of Antupara, was the first to shoot at
The monument; the arrow he sent could not pass
Beyond two *talas*. Next came Karnamali,

The king of Kinduka, whose arrow stopped after
Penetrating just one *tala*. All the kings
Tried their best to accomplish the task,
But their performance was below the mark.

At the time Mahisasura, who was travelling
In the mid-air, caught sight of the bride
From above. Enamoured of her beauty,
He descended there with a noise that resembled
The beating of the drum. His appearance was
Terrifying; he was huge, his hair and hands
Upraised, his teeth sticking out. He looked
Like Rahu swallowing the moon. Seeing
The demon, the kings began to flee. Mahisa
Reached the *swayambara* site while
Raktabirjya was shouting at the panicked
Kings to come back.

Mahisa told Chandra Naumi, "All the kings
Failed to prove their mettle. But I won't disappoint
You. I'll win the test and take Chandrabati
With me." Chandra Naumi replied, "We belong
To the clan of the Moon;
And you to the clan of demons.
Brahma, scared of you, gave you the boon.
How can I offer my daughter to a *chandal*?"
With a fiery temper, Mahisa picked up
His iron-bow, saying, "Now see, how I'm doing
It." Roaring like the sea, he took four arrows:
Brahma, *Rudra*, *Kashyap* and *Bajrasira*
And shot them from his bow with all his might.
The twang of the bowstring rocked the earth.

The four arrows pierced into the monument
Of one hundred and twenty-five *yojanas* wide
And flushed out at the other end. The gods
In heaven cheered him. King Chandra Naumi
Arranged his daughter's marriage with
Mahisasura on the fifth day of the bright
Fortnight of Bhadrab, which was followed
By celebrations. While leaving for his kingdom
With Chandrabati, Mahisasura held
Raktabirjya in deep embrace and sought
His help to further the expansion of his empire.
To Chandra Naumi he said, "Father! Allow
Raktabirjya and Bidulaksha to accompany me."
When he consented, he left with three *padmas*
Of warriors and the king's sons. With great
Pomp and ceremony, he entered his kingdom
With Chandrabati; the pair looked like Kama
And Rati. Raktabirjya and Bidulaksha were
Given a spectacular reception.'

9

Mahisasura's Conquest of Jambu Island

'It was a Sunday, the full moon day
Of Pausa, on which King Mahisa set out for
Jambu island, accompanied by Chamara, Bemala,
Kantimala, Raktabirjya, Bidulaksha and their
Respective armies. Hearing from their ministers
About the intrusion of the demons into their land,
All the kings in Jambu island shook with fear.
The demons went on a rampage in the places
They passed by, devouring the cattle and the brahmins
They found on their way. Looking as huge as
The Mandara mountain, they came riding lions,
Tigers and wild dogs. Raktabirjya, Bidulaksha,
Chamara, Bemala and Kantimala, heavily drunk,
Were babbling incoherently while drums, cymbals
And many other instruments were being played.
Brahma's boon had made them invincible;
Their bodies were immune to the strike of arrows.
As a supplement to drinks, they were eating the flesh

Of men, monkeys, horses and elephants. Having
No fear of death, they invaded and occupied
Kingdoms, such as Kashi, Kaushika, Kubuja
And Kanauja. Some of the kings fled in fear;
Others surrendered to Mahisa with all their wealth.
The idols of the gods were destroyed, be they
Of wood, stone or earth, *mandapas*, temples,
Religious places and heritage sites were desecrated.
They looked like a forest tossed by a storm. Kingdoms
Such as Gandhara, Parijataka, Pali and Baraswati,
Which came on their way to Sakhapur, were the most
Affected. Padmalabha, the king of Sakhapur,
Was a great devotee of Brahma.
The messengers informed, "O Lord! Mahisasura
Has arrived in your kingdom. After Singhala,
He is eyeing Jambu. All the kings have fled
To the forest, let alone confront him. If defeated,
Where would we go?" Commanding his army
To be on the alert for the impending peril,
The king got onto the watchtower and looked around.
What he saw at a distance was greatly disturbing.
In surprise, he told his minister, "I see the sea
Water has surged into the western territory,
Submerging it." The minister replied, "What you
Say sea water is, in fact, Mahisa's army, led
By his commanders. The flags and *chamars*
Look like storks in flight. The stamping
Of their feet sound like the roar of the sea."
In a few moments, Mahisa's army covered three
Yojanas and surrounded the fort. Sealing
The gates of the fort, the king warned the enemy
Not to proceed further. Being a descendant

Of the sun, he was blessed with Brahma's boon
For his unflinching devotion to him. Ananta,
His ancestor, had a son named Matangasura.
Matanga's son was Trisira and Trisira's son
Was Dundubhi. Dundubhi had a son called
Dumala and grandson, Kankasura. Kankasura's
Son was Dhankasura, grandson, Bakasura
And great-grandson, Bikrasura. Bikrasura
Had a son named Sukrasura. Sukrasura's
Son was Sulabha and grandson, Padmalabha.
Padmalabha had two sons, Bajralabha
And Siulabha.

The king was still shouting from inside
The fort, addressing Mahisasura, "See, both
Of us are of the same clan, same lineage
And same zodiac sign." Bidulaksha hit back,
"We don't care all that. Surrender to us if you
Think us as your own." Kantimala, in anger,
Commanded the soldiers to demolish the gates
With crowbars. Suddenly, the soldiers
Inside the fort started firing arrows at them.
Scared of their war cry, Mahisa's soldiers
Began to step back. Seeing it, Raktabirjya
Rose to the occasion, joined by Bidulaksha,
Kantimala, Chamara and Bemala. Those
Five commanders were as fearless as they were
Formidable. The arrows aimed at them from
Inside the fort harmed them the least; they
Broke into pieces as soon as they hit them.
With renewed vigour, Mahisa's soldiers
Dismantled the ramparts with crowbars,

And, entering the fort, challenged Padmalabha's
Army. A fierce battle ensued between the two
Opposing armies, with the clanging of swords
And maces. Padmalabha's army suffered
Heavy casualties, eighty thousand of them
Slain in a short time. The ground became muddy
With blood; the Sakhapur fort was severely
Damaged. The ramparts, watchtowers
And the palace were razed to the dust. Nevertheless,
The battle continued, neither of them willing
To concede defeat. Padmalabha's soldiers
Rained down arrows on the invaders to repel them.
Mahisa's commanders, who could conquer
Heaven effortlessly, put up a brave fight,
With eighty thousand soldiers led by Chamara
And Bemala. Furious, Kantimala hammered
Most of the enemy forces to death; a river
Of blood flowed in the Sakhapur fort. Seeing that
Kantimala was causing havoc among his soldiers,
The king challenged him with fifty-six crore
Of soldiers. When he accused him of slaying
His men unnecessarily, Kantimala told him,
"Don't you know how mighty Mahisasura is?
We conquered many kingdoms; no kings dared
Face us. We've defeated all the kings of Jambu
Island. One arrow is enough to finish you off.
Come with us to Mahisasura. He'll be pleased
To see you." Padmalabha replied, "After losing
So many innocent men, do you think, I'll pray
To him to draw up a peace treaty?" Saying so,
He commanded his soldiers to charge at the enemy.
Seeing this, Raktabirjya could not contain himself;

He held Padmalabha by the hair and killed him
With his sword. Then, he took his sons, Bajralabha
And Siulabha to King Mahisasura, and told him,
"Finding our soldiers slain in large numbers,
I killed King Padmalabha and brought his sons
To you. Though children, they're quite learned.
They're loyal to you. Let them rule Sakhapur
And remain obliged to you for all times to come."
Appreciating his suggestion, Mahisasura
Ordained them as kings of Sakhapur.'

Glory to you, O Brahman, born from
Ugratara's womb! O Creator of the universe!
You're the greatest of all the gods, so you're called
Mahadeva. Glory to you, O white-complexioned,
Mighty God! You're as vast as the sky and
The greatest of all yogis. Having the appearance
Of Bhrikuti, you present yourself as Sadashiva.
You swallowed poison for the well-being of others.
You ride a bull and play the *dambaru*. You've
No form; you're the embodiment of *maya*.
You burnt down Madana with fire from your
Eye. You're adorned with cobras, O sacred Soul!
You're the Lord of the universe; you're Triambika.
You wear your hair in three braids; you're
Adorned with sandalwood marks on your forehead.
You put on wooden sandals and carry Ganga
On your head. You're the Maker of everyone's
Destiny. You reside in every soul.
You're as limitless as the sea.
You're Maheswara. You're the beginning.
May my devotion to you be steadfast.

O Nilakantha!
Sarala Das prays at your lotus-feet.

The story of Mahisasura's conquest
Of Jambu island comes to an end.
O Noble ones!
How can I explain the ways of God?
I'm unlearned, lacking in qualifications
To compose a scripture. I'm only retelling
What is said in *Ayurveda*. I adore Goddess
Hingula, whose abode is in Jankherpur, as
A garland of *tulsi* around my neck. I've no
Merit of my own. It's she who induced me
To write. She is the eternal source of life
And energy. A great *yogini* herself, she
Destroys the wicked and protects the righteous.
As my Saviour, she instilled in me the wisdom
To accomplish my task. Looking as white as
Kunda flowers, her eyes are like the blue
Water-lilies. She is mighty; she is benevolent
Katyayani. O Noble ones!
I'm too feeble to write a scripture.
Whatever she dictates me in my slumber
At night, I put it in words in the morning.
She helps the poor and the needy as
A mother does to her children. She is
The Redeemer of human sufferings
She is *siddha* Sarala.
Sudramuni Sarala Das offers his prayers,
As holy as *tulsi*, at her feet.

10

Mahisasura's Battle with Shumbha and Nishumbha

King Parikshit told the sage, 'Mahisasura's
Invasion wreaked havoc throughout Jambu island.
Pray, tell me the events that followed it.' Sage
Shuka said, 'Listen! I'm telling you all that is
Recorded in the *Vishnu Purana*. Mahisasura
Subjugated kingdoms, such as Karnata, Gauda,
Malaba, Tirihuti, Chinhya, Mahachinhya,
Nepal, Baraswati, Kodha, Malara, Kauri,
Bangala, Bhota, Marahata, Lohita and Bhopal.
Some of the kings were held captive; others
Surrendered to him with all they possessed:
Elephants, horses, warriors, sons and relatives.

O Parikshit! On the south coast of the sea,
There was a city named Kulabati, ruled by
Two powerful kings, Shumbha and Nishumbha.
While they were young, they had been in
Meditation under a banyan tree, praying

To Brahma. For one thousand years
They lived on iron dust and another
Thousand years on water and *tulsi*. In
The third phase that continued for one thousand
Years, they meditated until their bodies collapsed
On the ground. Five thousand years passed by;
Their bodies were buried under the soil, dust
And termites piled on it.
In the next one thousand years
Brushes covered the place, leaving no trace
Of their bodies. After nine thousand years
Of their meditation, Brahma appeared before
Them. "I'm Brahma," he told them. "Ask for
Any boon you wish to have." As he took some
Water from his *kamandalu* and sprinkled
It over them the ground Shumbha and Nishumbha
Sprang to their feet and demanded from him
The proof of identity. Brahma showed his real
Form, sitting in a yogic posture with the four
Vedas in his four hands, and a divine glow
Emanating from his body. Pleased to see it,
They asked him to take a vow before awarding
The boon. When it was done, they prayed to him,
"O Lord, the lotus-seated One! Bless us that
We'll become immortal. The deluge cannot
Harm us. We'll live throughout the four Ages."
"So be it," Brahma said and left for his abode.

Being informed about it, Lord Indra
Hurried to Narayana and told him, "Brahma
Has rewarded Shumbha and Nishumbha with
The boon of immortality. What will happen

To the earth if these wicked demons are allowed
To prosper?" Worried, the Wheel-bearer, disguised
Himself as a frail, sickly old man, lay
On the path to the bathing ghat, obstructing
The way for Shumbha and Nishumbha to pass.
Seeing the old man in such deplorable condition,
The demons asked him who he was. The stranger
Opened his eyes, but he was too weak to speak
Anything. When they asked again, he said,
"I'm the king of Ananta island, the son of king
Nirakara. When the fear of death overcame me,
I meditated on Brahma for one lakh and sixty-seven
Years. Now I realize that all my labour is wasted.
Taking a vow, Brahma assured me that I'll live
As long as he lives and that no one can defeat
Me in war, not even Brahma, Rudra and Vishnu.
It has been five years and six months since
I received the boon. My hard-earned boon,
Unfortunately, turned futile. Since that day
I've been suffering from an incurable disease.
My only son was killed; my two wives were
Drowned to death. I lost everything I had.
O Shumbha and Nishumbha! One who is born
Must die. Even Brahma himself cannot
Escape death. Being the Creator, he is unable
To save himself. A body made of flesh
And blood is liable to wear out. I was a victim
Of his fraud and guile. See, how I am made
To lie here on this jungle path! I beg you for
Your help. I frantically need a yogi who
Can cure me. O Mahatmas! Brahma, whose
Abode is Yashobantipur, is a fraud. He couldn't

Manage with one head, so he had four heads
More. God, in anger, had slapped him across
His face that dislodged one of his heads. You
Can imagine what a creator he might be, from
The simple fact that he is the only God whom no one
Worships. His vices are many; he had an immoral
Relationship with a prostitute who gave birth
To Sage Basistha. He is incomplete in himself.
He is not worthy to be worshipped. He is despicable.
How sad, you spent, a good part of your life
Worshipping him!" While saying so, he let out
A wail and dropped dead there.

Taken by surprise, the demons were suspicious
Of Brahma's truthfulness. At Badrikashram,
They started meditation again, praying to Brahma.
Days passed by, still Brahma did not appear
Before them. Enraged, they left for heaven
And searched for him there. Their presence in
Heaven caused a panic among the gods, some
Of whom fled in fear. Sensing serious trouble,
Indra informed Brahma, "Shumbha and Nishumbha
Are looking for you here. The gods including
Yama have left heaven. We've to prevent them
At any cost." Enraged, Brahma came out with his
Bow and met the demons, who, seeing him furious,
Prepared themselves to attack him. Dumbstruck,
Brahma stood quietly and, before he could decide
What to do, the demons slapped him across his face,
That hurt him severely. Collecting himself,
He pronounced a curse on them, "O wicked demons!
You lost your reason and hit me on my face.

May your heads be burnt into ashes." Shocked,
They fell prostrate at his feet and prayed to him
To forgive them. They said, "We've committed
A great blunder by insulting you. We met an old man
Who told us you've deceived us. We are sorry.
Please forgive us." Brahma knew that the old man
Was no other than Hari. He told them, "He has told
You a lie. Though I am the giver of boons,
It is Damodara who faces the consequence.
As I said you'll live forever and defeat Brahma,
Vishnu and Rudra in war. One day you'll occupy
Heaven. But when you touch each other's
Head, you'll be burnt into cinders."

Returning to Kulabati, Shumbha and Nishumbha
Ruled their kingdom peacefully; they conquered
Many kingdoms and brought them under their sway.

One day, the messengers informed them,
"Mahisasura is ready to invade your kingdom.
He is the king of Singhala who has subjugated
Many kingdoms. Recently, he killed King Padmalabha
And ransacked Sakhapur. He has great commanders,
Such as Kantimala, Chamara, Bemala, Raktabirjya
And Dhumralochana." Hearing this, Shumbha
And Nishumbha proceeded to repel the invaders
With an army that spread over five *yojanas*.
Their warriors were equipped with weapons, such as
Spears, arrows, swords, clubs, crowbars, spades
And axes. Their war horses, of Iranian origin,
Could run faster than the wind. Drawing near
Mahisa's army, the troops of Kulabati raised

A war cry that frightened the enemy. Chamara, Bemala,
Kantimala and Bidulaksha were leading their army
From the front. A fierce battle ensued; the sound
Of clanging of swords filled the air. Bajranga
And Biraghanta, the commanders of Shumbha
And Nishumbha, launched an attack on Chamara
And Bemala. Bajranga slew many of Mahisa's
Soldiers who scattered like homeless birds,
Seeing it, Kantimala and Bidulaksha charged
At Biraghanta, while Raktabirjya showered one lakh
Arrows on Bajranga in vain. With nine lakh soldiers,
Chamara and Bemala battled against Biraghanta's
Five lakh strong army. Biraghanta using the arrow
Given to him by Parshurama in the Kamyak forest,
Wiped out one lakh of Mahisa's soldiers.
The battleground was soaked with blood
And the exchange of arrows darkened the sky.
In the meantime, Kantimala struck Biraghanta
With his mace that broke into two pieces.
On second attempt, he saw his mace was
Crushed into dust. As Biraghanta's attack
Gained momentum, Mahisa's soldiers retraced
Five *yojanas* back. Mahisasura retreated
To Vindhyagiri hills. Seeing the enemy dispersed,
Shumbha and Nishumbha returned to Kulabati.'

Glory to God, the blue-complexioned one!
Since the day Sribaccha kicked at your chest,
You have been called Sribacchi. A lover
Of devotees, you are the enchanter of the *gopis*.
O Lord! Your creation is incomprehensible.
I wish to sing your glory all my life. This earthly

Life is a noose around my neck. It's you who can
Unhitch me. Driven by self-pride, I revel in
Falsehood. Remove the illusion that shrouds
My mind. Day and night I think on you,
O Redeemer of my soul! Brahma, Indra, the Moon,
The Sun and all the gods are like the beads
Of the garland around your neck.
I bow to you, O Narayana! In this transitory
World, you're the one who is eternal. O Lord!
You and your creation are inseparable from
Each other like the moon and the *chakora*.
I could feel your presence by dedicating myself
To you with single-minded devotion.
I chant your name day and night.
The maimed, the helpless, the ignorant
And the sinners – all of them achieved salvation
Only by chanting your name. Thus says
Sudramuni Sarala Das, wearing a *tulsi* garland
And bowing at your sacred feet.

O Learned ones!
Remember, Sarala Chandi of Jankherpur
Is the only Saviour!
Once, wishing to see Lord Vishnu,
Sage Manu went to Vaikuntha, but Jaya
And Bijaya, who stood watch at the gate,
Did not let him in. He requested them again
And again with folded hands, but it was in
Vain. Seeing his frail body, they gave him
A push that sent him hurling in the air
Nine thousand *yojanas* away. Collecting himself,
He returned to heaven again. Singing from

The Vedas, he requested them to allow him go
Inside. Instead, they let out a stream
Of abuse at him. Flying into a fury, the sage
Cursed them, 'Being mere gatekeepers of heaven,
You dared hit a sage, as frail and weak
As I am. May you be born as demons in your
Next birth.' Shocked at the curse, they
Prayed to him, 'O Brahma's son! O Manu!
We committed a great blunder not knowing
Who you are. Kindly tell us how to expiate
Our sin.' The sage told them, 'For your offence,
You'll be born as demons. You can restore
Your position by your devotion to Vishnu.
You'll be Krishna's enemy and return
To Vaikuntha after three births. In your
First birth, you'll be known as Hiranya
And Hiranaksha, in which you'll kidnap
Vishnu's consort. In the second, you'll be
Ravana and Kumbhakarna. You'll kidnap
Sita and Sri Rama will chop your head.
In the third, you'll be born as Dantabakra
And Sisupala. You'll kidnap Rukmini
And be slain by Narayana. For all
The three births you'll be kidnappers
Of women, before you return to Vaikuntha.'

Cursed by Manu, Jaya and Bijaya
Were born as demons. With their disappearance,
The gates of Vaikuntha remained unattended.
Being informed about Manu's curse, Vishnu
Sent for Brahma's son. He held Manu
Responsible for it and told him, 'The punishment

Meted out to my gatekeepers is much greater
Than their crime. For the injustice you did
To them, you'll be born as man on the earth.'
Manu said benignly, 'In obedience to your
Command, I'll be born as man. In my first
Birth, I'll please Goddess Girija and hear
Vishnu's story from her. In my second birth,
I'll be known as Kalidas who will receive
The blessings of Saraswati. In the third,
I'll be Sarala Das who will devote himself
To Sarala Chandi. With her blessings I'll write
The *Ramayana* first, then the *Mahabharata*
And thirdly, *Sri Bhagavata*.'

Thus says Sudramuni Sarala Das, praying
At the feet of Sarala Chandi of Jankherpur.

11

Mahisasura Loses the Battle

'Listen, O Parikshit!
May your sins be redeemed by listening
To *Sri Bhagavata*.

When it became morning, both the armies
Started for the battlefield, Shumbha and Nishumbha
From Kulabati city and Mahisa from the Vindhyagiri
Mountain. The battle ensued; a rain of arrows
Poured down from the skies. Raktabirjya,
Biraghanta, Chamara and Bemala led the attack,
Brandishing their maces. Seeing Raktabirjya
Full of fire, Shumbha and Nishumbha hit him
With their unwieldy maces. Raktabirjya
And Shumbha, holding each other's arm
Boxed and wrestled, each trying to outclass the other.
Raktabirjya fell to the ground and passed out.
Next, Shumbha thrashed Chamara with his mace
That sent him sprawling onto the ground, unconscious.
Kantimala rushed to the spot to retaliate, but

Was soon overpowered. Seeing his commanders
Beaten, one after another, Mahisa himself took over
The responsibility. In a tearing rage, Shumbha
And Nishumbha, as huge as the Mandara
Mountain, stretched their
Hands to catch Mahisa, like Rahu attempting
To swallow the sun. Jayasingha, Bajrasingha
And Mahisasura, the threesome, unitedly combated
With them, raining down arrows on Shumbha,
Who, with his mace, broke Mahisa's chariot
Into pieces. A fresh battle started between Shumbha
And Raktabirjya; the earth shook under
The weight of their feet. Mahisa attacked Nishumbha,
But while hitting him, his mace broke and fell
Into pieces. Seeing Shumbha running towards
Him aggressively, Mahisa decided to pull out
Of the battle. Shumbha blocked his way
And asked, "Who are you? Why did you trespass
On my land? Don't you know the sun and the wind
Dare not intrude into my kingdom? How could
You enter here?" Mahisa replied, "I'm the king
Of Singhala, my kingdom spreads over forty lakh
Yojanas. I conquered the islands, such as Karancha,
Kunja and Chandra. Raktabirjya, Chamara
And Bemala are the kings who surrendered
To me. Sage Narada told me about your land
And was full of praise for it. That tempted
Me to invade it. Now that I'm defeated,
I surrender to you." Pleased, Shumbha embraced
Him, and as a sign of friendship, offered him
The kingdom of Kulabati.

Days wore on. One day Narada, the Messenger
Of heaven, appeared there, clad in white and singing
And dancing. He used to speak the truth, but in
A twisted manner, for which he was liked by all.'

Glory to Narayana, the Saviour of mankind!
You've no beginning, nor end. You're the Creator
Of all living beings. Brahma, who is Holiness
Incarnate, is born from you. It is you who instructs
Me to write. Vyasa wrote down your words
And I followed him. You're the source of all wisdom.
You're Jagannath! For redeeming the sins
Of Kali Yuga, your face has turned black.
One who thinks on you, is free from all sins.
Sarala Chandi of Jankherpur, Krupajal's
Daughter, and Lord Shiva's consort inspires me
To write, and I do so by hearing from Vyasa.
Thus says Sarala Das, bowing at the feet
Of the benevolent Goddess. Forgive my ignorance.
O Learned Ones! Give up all distractions;
Keep chanting Krishna's name. Talking about him
Or hearing about him will lead you on the path
Of righteousness and fulfil all your wishes.

'Sage Narada adorned his seat and enquired
About everyone. Greatly impressed by the city
Of Kulabati, he told Shumbha and Nishumbha,
"Your kingdom is beautiful and prosperous. No other
Demon king has been able to build a city such as this.
It's well protected by four high mountains: Ratnagiri
In the east, Singhagiri in the west, Kundagiri in
The south and Vindhyagiri in the north. No other city

Can be equal to it in majesty and richness, except
For Amaravati. But it doesn't have the four things
That Amaravati has. They are Airavata, the elephant;
Rambha, the *apsara*; Uccaihsraba, the horse;
And Parijata, the flower."

So saying, the sage left, but his words
Kept haunting the demon kings. "We've achieved
Everything with our might, but not these four
Things the sage had mentioned," they thought.
In order to get them as soon as possible,
They ordered the ministers, "Send our messengers
To Amaravati immediately with our letter."'

12

Mahisasura's Letter to Indra

'"Glory to Sun-god, Kashyap's son, who has
No beginning, nor end; who is the source
Of eternal joy and the Lord of the fourteen worlds.
Mahisasura of Simhika's family, the Light of Rahu's
Clan, prays at your feet.

Letter from the Monarch of all the kingdoms:
The netherworld and all that the eyes can see,
Blessed by Brahma, Singhala his abode, the Lord
Of the gods, men, *gandharvas*, *dakshas*, *kinnars*,
Planets, Yama's messengers, beasts and demons,
The ruler of all *dikpalas* and all castes. He is Garuda
For the world of *nagas*, the omnipotent, the epitome
Of the three basic attributes of the creation, and the master
Of scriptures and warfare. Being mightier with Brahma's
Boon, he gained authority over Yama, King of Death.
He conquered kingdoms, such as Jambu, Singhala,
Koshala, Chandra, the nine islands and the seven seas.
He defeated kings, such as Raktabirjya, Chamara,

Bemala, Biraghanta, Dhumralochana, Kantimala,
Chanda, Munda, Shumbha and Nishumbha.
He has taken control over Chudanga, Kashi, Kaushika,
Nepal, Pasupatra, Gauda, Gajana, Tihudi, Malab,
Gujjar, Magadha, Macchya, Sakha, Saurastra, Kanchi,
Mahendra, Marahata, Bijantaka, Yamuna, Saveri, etc.
He is Yogi of *yogis*; he is Managovinda.
Mahisasura commands Indra of Amaravati
To present himself before him with Airavata,
Rambha, Parijata and Uccaihsraba."

Shumbha and Nishumbha ordered
Two of his messengers, Sahasra and Prasasta,
To carry the letter to heaven and fetch Indra forthwith.
With the king's letter, they set out for Amaravati.

Sensing the arrival of the demons, Narada
Informed Indra, "O Lord! Mahisasura has sent
His messengers here to fetch you." Indra showed
Least concern about it, but it made his inside
Twist in alarm. He felt a tremor of panic.
Just then, both the demons reached there
And shouted at him, "O Indra! Mahisasura,
The Lord of the three worlds, commands you
To leave your throne and meet him at once".
Their hurtful behaviour was too much for Indra
To take in. One of the *gandharvas* present there
Held the demons by the hair and struck them with
An axe that sent their bodies sprawling
Onto the ground, cut in half. Shocked at
What happened, Narada asked, "Why did you kill
The messengers? Killing a messenger

Is as great a sin as killing a brahmin.' To him
Indra replied firmly, "I'm the king of the gods.
I'm Jambubhedi as I killed Jambu, the demon.
Who should I fear?"

O Parikshit! On a Sunday, the second day
Of the bright fortnight of the month of Chaitra,
Shumbha and Nishumbha held a meeting
Of their ministers and courtiers in the presence
Of Mahisasura's minister, Andhaka, who could
Tell the past, present and future.' King Parikshit
Asked the sage, 'How is it that Mahisasura, the king
Of nine islands, chose a blind man as his minister?
What is the rationale behind it?' The sage
Explained, 'Andhaka was the grandson of Raksha
And Bhaksha, the son of Praheti and the brother
Of Sajabali. He was brought up by Mahisasura's
Mother in his childhood. Displeased with Mahisa's
Wicked behaviour, he once cautioned him,
"You've earned a great fortune with your might.
Your wrongful actions will bring your end soon."
Enraged, Mahisa plucked out his eyes. In severe
Pain, he rolled on the ground, praying to God for
Help. Moved by his prayer, Lord Shiva arrived
There, riding a bull. He asked him, "What happened?
I couldn't stand your painful cry. So I came here."
Andhaka replied, "I'm the son of Praheti of the clan
Of Raksha and Bhaksha and the great-grandson
Of Suraksha. I'm Mahisa's uncle. Objecting to
His wicked manners, I advised him to correct himself.
In anger, he plucked out my eyes.' The Lord
Consoled him, "Both of us are called Birupaksha.

So, you're my namesake. That makes us
Friends to each other. I'll restore your eyesight."
Andhaka interrupted, "I don't want to see what
He does or not. I'll be happy to live as a blind man.
If you're so kind, grant me the power to see the
Past, present and future, even without eyesight.
That'll qualify me to be his minister." Pleased,
The Lord granted him an all-encompassing vision,
That nothing will hide from his view. This is
How he came to be known as Andhaka.

Shumbha and Nishumbha asked Andhaka,
"Tell us the news of our messengers who had been
To Amaravati long ago." Andhaka replied, "Incensed
By Mahisa's command, Indra killed both of them."
Fuming with anger, Shumbha and Nishumbha
Started for heaven in a chariot pulled by
One thousand lions. Being informed of their
Arrival by Narada, Indra, fully armed, rode
Airavata and proceeded with other gods to repel
The demons. As they met with each other,
Indra cried out, "O Shumbha and Nishumbha!
You rule the earth; I rule heaven. We are brothers.
Why are you hostile to me?" The demons replied,
"O Indra! Mahisasura is the conquerer
Of the world. True, the gods and the demons are
Brothers. But you made our relationship miserable
By killing Jambu, the demon. My king had sent
Two of his messengers to you. You killed them
Without any reason. How dare you do it?
We won't return unless you hand us over
Airavata, Parijata, Rambha and Uccaihsraba.

You've committed a grievous error by killing
The messengers. We are demons, still we are scared
Of doing anything unholy. People do such things
When their end is near." To them, Indra said,
"I'm the king of gods. Who do I care?" Shumbha
Warned him, "You're choosing a wrong path.
Will you obey Mahisasura's orders or not?"
"Let me talk to Brahma first. I'm Indra because
Of him, you're great because of his blessing."
So saying, he left for Brahma's abode. Soon
The demons occupied Indra's throne
And kidnapped an *apsara* called Kamasena.

Finding Brahma in deep meditation,
Indra had to wait for nine *dandas*, which was
Equal to nine thousand years for the gods.
In the meantime, the demons had taken control
Of Indra's abode and continued to rule heaven.
All the planets and *dikpalas* were at their service,
Doing errands for them. Since Yama had fled
In fear, there was no fear of death any longer.
No one died on the earth; everyone was happy
And fearless. Surprised at the changes,
Mahisa asked Andhaka, "How come, the gods
Are ruling the heaven so successfully?"
Andhaka replied, "When Narada told them
To fetch four things from heaven, such as
Airavata, Rambha, Parijata and Uccaihsraba,
Shumbha and Nishumbha sent messengers
To Indra to get them. Indra killed the messengers,
And to avenge their death, Shumbha and Nishumbha
Occupied Amaravati and drove away Indra.

At their command, it only rains at night. Yama
Has fled heaven, so no one dies these days,
The sages and brahmins, being immortal, praise
Your lordship with respect." Delighted, Mahisa
Took off his crown, earrings and necklaces
And ordered Chamara and Bemala to offer those
To Shumbha and Nishumbha for their spectacular
Achievement. Chamara and Bemala, followed
By nine lakh soldiers, reached Amaravati. Offering Mahisa's
presents to Shumbha and Nishumbha,
They told them, "Mahisa has been pleased to offer
You his ornaments in appreciation of your
Brave work. He has also asked you to continue
As kings of heaven."'

King Parikshit, praying at the sage's feet,
Implored, 'Lord Indra had left for Brahma's
Abode in haste. What did Brahma say to Indra?'
Shuka replied, 'Listen! After his meditation was
Over, Brahma opened his eyes.' Parikshit interrupted,
'Why does Brahma meditate? He is the Creator
And the wisest of all. Why should he meditate?'
The sage replied, 'Listen carefully. He has created
Four kinds of living beings, eighty-four lakhs
In number. Every day he has to look after them.
It's his duty to ensure that everything runs smoothly.
He has four faces and eight eyes; he uses them
For this purpose. For all this, he requires
An eighteen-*danda* meditation every day.'

Glory to the Progenitor of gods, the Creator
Of crores of Universe! He uses his left head for

Singing *Atharvaveda*, the back one for *Rigveda*,
The one at the right for *Samaveda* and the front one
For *Jajurveda*. He is Brahman himself. Thus says
Sudramuni Sarala Das, bowing at Brahma's feet.

x x x

Sage Shuka, Vyasa's son, narrated all that
Happened between Brahma and Indra, as told
By Brahma to Vyasa.

'Seeing Indra in Brahma's abode, the *gandharvas*
And the *apsaras* informed him, "Once you left
Amaravati, Shumbha and Nishumbha took possession
Of your abode. They kidnapped two of your *apsaras*:
Kamasena and Mohini. Chamara and Bemala have
Joined them with an army of demons." His meditation
Ended, Brahma opened his eyes and saw Indra
Bowing at his feet. When he asked him what
Brought him there, the king of Amaravati said,
"O Lord! It seems you don't care for us at all.
You made me the king of heaven. Let me inform
You that Mahisasura, Kapilasingha's son,
Has occupied Amaravati. He had sent his messengers
To me demanding Airavata, Parijata, Rambha
And Uccaihsraba. When I refused, they insulted
Me with hurtful words. In anger, I killed both
The messengers. Seeking revenge, Shumbha
And Nishumbha arrived here with a large army.
They turned me out of my abode and kidnapped
Two *apsaras*: Kamasena and Mohini. Empowered
By your boon, Mahisa became the monarch
Of the three worlds." Saying so, he took off his royal

Robes and jewellery and put it before him.
Brahma advised him, "Let Shumbha and Nishumbha
Be in Amaravati. You stay in my abode with
The *gandharvas* and the *apsaras*."

It was a Saturday, the sixth day of the bright
Fortnight of the month of Bhadrab. Shumbha
And Nishumbha, with their army, proceeded
To Alakapuri to carry out a raid on it, Chamara
And Bemala following them with their troops.
Hearing the voice of Providence that warned him
Of the arrival of the demons, Kubera was worried.
"I can never beat them in war," he thought. With
Some precious jewellery and robes meant for
The coronation of the gods, he left his abode.
After robbing Alakapuri, the demons chased
Kubera who was running away. Seeing that
He is being followed, Kubera threw the robes
And jewellery and disappeared into Nairutapur.
Collecting those things, Chamara and Bemala
Posted some guards in Alakapuri and returned.

Arriving at Jenabati, they met Mahisasura,
Laying the booty out before him. It included
The jewels collected from the sea when, years ago,
The sea was being churned. Mahisa adorned
Himself with the robes and ornaments that Indra
Used to wear, and the rest, he gave away among
His commanders. Raktabirjya, Biraghanta
And Bidulaksha put the necklaces of the gods
Around their necks. All of Mahisa's followers
Revelled in drinking, dancing and playing musical

Instruments. At Mahisa's command, the charioteer
Decorated the chariot with nine kinds of gems
And yoked lions to it. As Mahisa adorned
The chariot, it flew into the sky at the speed
Of the wind. The gods, *gandharvas*, *dakshas*
And *kinnars*, whoever were there in heaven fled
In fear. With his followers, Mahisasura entered
Amaravati, where he was received warmly.
Shumbha and Nishumbha offered him the coronation
Attire of Indra. They offered gems to Ratkabirjya,
Andhaka, Biraghanta, Kantimala, Chanda, Munda,
Bidulaksha, Bhaskar, Surabara, Bhagava,
Birabahu, Lohasura, Kanka, Dhanka, Kalanala,
Bahu, Subahu, Chanda, Prachanda Umura,
Dumura, Sukha, Durmukha, Gila, Mahagila,
Tadaka and Bimukha. Praising Shumbha
And Nishumbha, Mahisa said, "It's for you that
The entire heaven became ours." He ordained
Kalaketu as the king of Sanjibanipura.
Biraghanta became the king of Hemabantapura;
The charge of Hiranyagarvapura was left
To Bidulaksha and Chamara and Bemala
Became the custodians of Alakapuri.

Realizing the gravity of the situation,
Narada informed Brahma, "Mahisasura has captured
The entire heaven. He has placed Chanda and Munda
In charge of the nether world and Jalataranga
Is made the king of Barunapura. Thus, the positions,
Earlier held by the gods, are now gone to the hands
Of the demons." Shocked to learn that the Moon,
The Sun, the Wind and Baruna were turned out

Of their abode, Brahma decided to meet Narayana
With all the gods. They set out for the Milky Sea:
Brahma on a swan, Indra on Airavata, Yama
On a buffalo, Shiva on a bull, the Wind on a deer,
Brihaspati on a swan and Kamadeva on
Uccaihsraba. Their consorts too joined them.
Thirty-three crores of gods reached the Milky Sea
Where Narayana lay supinely on the coils
Of the great cobra, Birajachakra, Lakshmi
And Narmada sitting beside him. On Brahma's
Request, Narmada played her *veena* with
Sweet notes to awake Narayana. Arising
From sleep, he wiped his eyes and found the gods,
Lying prostrate before him. There was a gloomy
Silence all around; despair was writ large
On every face. When he wanted to know why
They were there, Brahma said politely, "You forgot
All of us, lying here, free from worries". Vishnu
Replied, "Being the Creator, who do you fear?"
The gods complained, "The atrocity of the demons
Bear heavily on us. The Earth is bleeding through
Her nose." The Fire, the Moon and the Sun added,
"Mahisasura's oppression has become too much
To take in. He usurped our kingdom and ill-treated
Us. The demons took away our *apsaras*. They are
Ill-advised by Andhaka. Kubera fled in fear.
They sucked Baruna's abode dry. They robbed
The kingdom of *nagas*. We suffered immensely
And you did nothing to protect us.
Finding no other alternative, we came
To you, seeking help."

Annoyed, Sri Hari said, "O Brahma!
Why did you grant such a boon without considering
Its consequence? O Shiva! You're called Tripurari
As you have killed Tripura, the demons. Why couldn't
You eliminate Shumbha and Nishumbha?"
Shiva replied, "Pleased with Mahisa's devotion,
Brahma granted them the boon that
None of the gods, men, *nagas*, monkeys,
Bears and demons will take their life. Neither Yama
Nor the deluge will put them to death. The Wind won't
Drift them away and the Fire won't burn them.
The anger of the gods and the curses of sages
Won't impact them. O Lord! I'm undone!"
Narayana said, "It means he won't die
In my hands. The demons know it well; so
They are not afraid of me." Hearing this, the Earth
Cried bitterly, "How I wish I sank into
The netherworld! Let the world perish."
The Moon and the Sun refused
To shine in the sky; they would prefer to stay
In the Milky Sea and serve at Narayana's feet.
The Wind said, "I'll stop blowing; let the living beings
Suffocate to death." Looking at Narayana's face,
All the gods wailed and wept. They were saying,
"You're our only Saviour. We have become
Slaves in our own homes. We have been robbed
Of our power and position." A howl of grief
Filled the night air.

It was the eighth day of the dark fortnight
Of Ashwin. It was late evening when Mahisa
Disguised as a buffalo, was skulking at the foot

Of the Meru mountain. Suddenly he heard
Narayana's voice coming from the mountain.
He was conspiring with the gods to kill
Mahisasura. In a mad fit, he struck the mountain
With his horns that made it crumble.
This infuriated the thirty-three
Crore of gods present there; their faces
Turned red and their eyes glinted in anger.
The fire from their eyes spread in all directions,
As if the seven worlds were in flames.
Scared, Mahisa retraced his steps.
He told Shumbha and Nishumbha,
"Do you know, Uncle, what the gods did? While
Travelling in the dark, I heard them planning
For my death. Command the demons to attack
The gods mercilessly." Shumbha and Nishumbha
Replied that the gods had taken shelter in Brahma's
Abode. "Demolish Brahma's abode, then appoint
Chanda and Munda rulers of Yashobantipura."
Shumbha and Nishumbha protested, "For all that
You achieved, you owe it to Brahma. How'll you
Go against him for no reason?" Mahisasura
Roared out, "If he is our father, how does he think
Ill of us? A father, unable to protect his family,
Deserves to die." "Where did the gods go from
The Meru mountain?" they asked. Mahisa replied,
"I don't know. I left the place at the sight of fire."
Hearing this, Chanda and Munda decided to go
To Meru mountain and launch an assault
On Brahma's abode.

On second thoughts, Mahisasura decided
To consult Andhaka before taking any measure

Against Brahma. Returning to his kingdom,
He told Andhaka about all that had happened.
Andhaka told him, "You've done a grievous
Mistake. You usurped Amaravati and carried away
Lakshmi on your head. Your ancestors, such as
Tripura, Taraka, Raksha and Bhaksha, never
Invaded heaven." Hearing this, Mahisa was
Scared, but sported his pride as usual. He ordered
His commanders, Sindhu and Upasindhu,
To guard the north coast. He cautioned them,
"In case the gods attempt to hide in the sea,
Catch hold of them." In addition, he deployed
Jalataranga inside the sea. He asked
Bidulaksha to suck the Milky Sea dry. He sent
Chamara and Bemala to empty the Nila Sea.
He asked Krutantaka to suck the waters
Of the Ikshu Sea. He commanded Mukha
And Durmukha, the two brothers, to empty
The Kshara Sea. Chanda and Munda were
Asked to suck all the water of the Salt Sea.
This way, he ordered his commanders
To ensure that all the seas were dried up.
He decided to attack Brahma's abode on
The tenth day of the month.'

Hearing this, the king of Kuru's clan asked
The sage, 'What did the gods do when the place
Was ablaze?' Sage Shuka replied, 'Listen to
The story of Sri Durga now. That will wash away
All your sins. To propitiate God of Fire, the gods
Recited *mantras*, each of them contributing
Their inherent powers to it. The fires broke out
In a massive shape, spreading across heaven that

Forced the demons to return to Jenabatipura,
All the gods prayed to God of Fire in chorus:

"Glory to you, O Fire!
Your power and purity are well proven.
Your flames touch the top of the universe.
O Mahatma! You're impartial, terrible
And full of energy. You've no beginning, nor
End. You can easily penetrate heaven. You're
God of gods, formless and incomprehensible.
You make the impossible possible. You're *siddha*.
You're in a state of ecstatic frenzy. You're
Merciful to the impoverished and the needy.
You're a column of nectar that pierces the sky.
All gods are born from you. You're uncommon.
There is no end to your appetite. You can consume
The whole world, and still be hungry. You're kind.
You're the Creation. You're Brahman.
Your benevolence will continue as long as the sun
And the moon exist. You live in the bowels
Of the earth, nether regions and heaven. You're
The Lord of all. You fear none. You're above
All chants and *mantras*. You can make yourself
Invisible in a moment. You're self-born,
Worshipped by gods and sages. Ayurveda,
Jyotirveda, Dhanurveda, Sisuveda and Gayatri
Are the five armours that make you invincible.
You destroy creation after creation effortlessly
And also recreate them. You've no girdle, but
Only a belly, large enough to contain the Creation.
You're Narayana. You're the Sun. You're Baiswanara.
You're the wisest and the holiest. You're Yogi

Of *yogis*. You're born from the sea. O Lord!
You're the most ancient of all gods. You're known
For your forbearance. When Vishnu and Shiva
Are worshipping you, who am I to describe
Your greatness?"'

Sage Shuka said, 'Listen, King Parikshit!
Moved by Brahma's prayer, his sister appeared
From the roaring fire, sparkling like a gem. Her
Radiance belied her beauty. She had one head,
Two legs and one thousand hands. She was Katyayani;
She was Kamakshi; she was Tarini, the great Vaishnavi,
Calm and gratified. Seeing her gigantic figure,
The gods were scared. Brahma, Vishnu, Maheswar
And the Moon lay prostrate before her in respect.
Thirty-three crore of gods bowed at her feet.

Her forehead was made of the fire of
Brahma; her face of that of Narayana;
Her teeth of Maheswar's; eyes of God of Fire,
Nose of Indra; radiance of her face of Aditya;
Tongue of the Moon, cheeks of Yama; chest of Kubera;
Armpit of God, the Formless; navel of Sanaka;
The folds on her abdomen of Ashwini Kumar;
The nose-rings of Yama and Brihaspati; thighs
Of Prajapati; feet of Ananta Basuki; toes of
The nine planets and Bhrigu; fingers of *kunda*
Buds; the back of Hemavanta; the hair of the stars;
The belly of Baruna; the water in her body of Rain;
Her one thousand hands of forty-nine winds;
Her words of Yama and her holiness of Vaishnavas.

She was as wise as Brahma; as enchanting
As Kamadeva; as warlike as Krishna; as learned
As Brihaspati; as boastful as Indra; as glorious
As the Moon; as radiant as the Sun; as cruel as Yama;
As forbearing as the Earth; as swift as the Wind;
As sacred as the Meru; as charming as the Rain;
As solemn as Baruna, as captivating as Parvati
And as resolute as Kumara.

Listen, O King! She was born from the fire,
Contributed by each of the gods; her nature was
An amalgam of their attributes. Suddenly
The voice of Providence was heard from above:
She is the one who will save the world from
The powers of evil, so she is named Durga.

Brahma, Vishnu and Maheswar prayed to her
With folded hands, "Glory to you, O Katyayani,
The Benevolent One! You restore order after violence.
You're the epitome of goodness,
And the Saviour of mankind.
O Durga! O Mangala!
You protect us from evil."'

How can an ignorant child as I am, describe
You whom the gods worship? O Noble ones!
You learnt how she was born. By pleasing her,
You can achieve righteousness, riches, fulfilment
Of wishes and salvation. Chant her name,
And your misfortunes are removed and you're free
From the bondage of time. She will save you
From the fear of disease and death. You can

Ward the evil spirits off. Those who are issueless,
Will be blessed with children. Worship her
From the bright fortnight of Ashwin till
The ninth day. She will bless you with
A long life, wealth and son – everything.
O Mother Durga! Only you can save us from
Greed, attachment and worldly worries.
O Mother! Reside in me all my life.
Thus says Sudramuni Sarala Das, praying
For her mercy.

x x x

'O Parikshit! Pleased with the devotion
Of the gods, the Goddess, calm and composed, asked,
"O gods! You pray to me so benignly. Tell me,
What are you worrying about?" Vishnu motioned
For Brahma to speak. Who, with folded hands,
Gave a full account of the inside story.

"Mother! Ten of the sixty daughters of Daksha
Prajapati, were married to Yama. They were
Tanu, Bhanu, Medha, Sraddha, Sruti, Mruti,
Shanti, Sumedha, Buddhi and Trusti. Uma married
Shiva and I married Savitri. Nirabati was married
To Baruna; Swaha and Sudha to Fire. Tara
And Hara married Brihaspati and Kubera
Respectively. To Aditya, Daksha offered Samjna
And to the Moon, twenty-seven of his daughters.
Hema did not marry; she spent her life
As a *yogini*. Kashyap married
Thirteen of them, such as Diti, Aditi, Binata,

Kadru, Kala, Anala, Gandharvi, Daksha, Raksha,
Arasti, Gruhija, Suravi and Simhika. To Aditi
The gods were born and to Diti, Pabana and Sampati,
Kadru gave birth to snakes and Binata to Garuda.
Gandharvas were born to Gandharvi, and *dakshas*
And *kinnars* to Daksha. Raksha gave birth to
Quadrupeds, such as elephants, horses, bears
And deer. To Kala, Kalapurusa was born and to Anala,
The mountains. Suravi gave birth to the cattle
And Gruhija to the best of men. To Arasti were born
The untouchables and to Simhika, a son called Rahu.
Aditya chopped him in half for his wickedness.
The lower part of his body was named Ketu.
Ketu's son, Jambu, while trying to capture the Sun,
Was slain by Indra. Jambu's son was Hiranyakashyapa
And grandsons, Raksha and Bhaksha.

In Satya Yuga, a series of fights went on between
The gods and the demons, in which many demons
Were slain by Narayana. They included Heti and
Praheti, the sons of Raksha and Bhaksha, Bajranga's
Son, Hiranyakachapa, grandson, Bajrakapacha,
His sons, Andhaka and Tripura. Tripura's son,
Sambu was killed by Kamadeva for kidnapping
Bedamati. Sambu's son, Jalataranga died
In the hands of Vishnu. Sankhasura, Jalataranga's
Son, made off with the Vedas written by me. Vishnu,
In the guise of a fish, took his life. Jagannath,
Disguised as a tortoise, killed Sankhasura's
Son, Abani. Abani's son, Hiranaksha, was
Slain by a boar, the incarnation of Vishnu.
His son, Keshi, was put to death by Keshaba.

He also killed Keshi's son, Amaya. Vishnu,
Incarnated as Narasimha, killed Amaya's
Son, Hiranyakashyapa. Krishna killed his son,
Bailochana, by tricking him in the guise of a woman.
Incarnated as Bamana, Vishnu trampled Bali,
Bailochana's son, to the netherworld. Bali's son,
Maya was killed by Krishna in a battle.
Hanumanta killed Maya's son, Amaya. Amaya's
Son, Tadakasura was slain by Karttikeya.
Tadaka's son was Lohasura, his son was
Bajrasingha and grandson, Kapilasingha.
Mahisasura is Kapilasingha's son who prayed
To me for thousands of years with greatest devotion.
Overwhelmed by it, I blessed him with immortality,
I assured him that he will defeat Brahma, Vishnu,
Shiva, the Wind, the Moon and the Sun in war.
He conquered the three worlds. He made
Bajrasingha the king of Padma island and Mahaketu
Of Chandra island. He appointed Subahu the ruler
Of Kusha island, while he himself ruled Singhala
Island. He made Bhaskar the king of Karancha island,
Shumbha and Nishumbha kings of Jambu island
And Jalataranga the king of Barunapura. Bhumidahana
Ruled the netherworld, and Sindhu
And Upasindhu remained in charge of the north
And the west. Kalanjan became the king of forests,
Bajraketu of mountains and Subanu of Nishadapura.
O mother! Now Shumbha and Nishumbha have
Occupied Amaravati; Biraghanta has become
The king of Yashobantipura, Raktabirjya
Of Hiranyagarvapura, Bhaskar of the abode of Fire,
And Chanda and Munda of my abode. O mother!

The demons have usurped the three worlds.
Mahisasura has terrorized all of us. O Mother!
You're Brahmayani, Indrayani, Narayani, Matangi,
Rudrayani, Tarini, Samayani, Maheswari, Mahamaya,
Baseli, Ugratara, Katyayani, Bhabani, Tripura,
Bijaya, Ambika, Madhavi, Kankali, Betali, Kalika,
Bhairabi, Chandi, Chamundi, Prachanda, Barahi,
Bikarali, Kamaseni, Kritanteki, Nagari, Kamakshi,
Sadhabi, Pingalakshi, Adityayi, Marutri,
Dakshinai, Uttarayani, Paschimai, Karatai,
Chhaya, Maya, Annapurna, Kumari, Bikatai
And Ghorarupai! O Mother! You've one thousand
Hands; you can also take one thousand forms
At will!" So saying, Brahma and the gods bowed
To her, which pleased her most.'

Thus says Sarala Das, the poet,
Serving at Sri Durga's feet.

x x x

'Listen, Parikshit!
Taking pity on the gods, Katyayani told
Brahma to ask for any boon he liked to have.
Brahma, respectfully, begged her,
"On behalf of the thirty-three crore of gods
Devoted to you, I pray for Mahisasura's
Death." The Goddess assured him, "I'll
Make every effort to kill the demon." Saying so,
She stretched out her hands. Vishnu gave his conch,
Wheel and mace in her hands, Brahma his *kamandalu*,
Dambaru, *pasupata* and *pinaki* bow and Indra
His *ajagaba* bow. The gods, who were Aditi's sons,

Gave their earrings as round as the sun and a gem
Necklace. Biswadevas gave her a gem that could
Dispel the thickest darkness and a sword.
The Moon offered *amritasara* and *hemachakra*
Snare, the Sky the blue wheel, Yama the death-snare
And Kamadeva his five hypnotizing arrows. Bhrigu
Gave her a potful of intoxicating juice,
A battleaxe and mace. The Almighty gave her
Chakradanda. The Wind gave her a wheel, ever rotating.
Hemavanta presented the *parvata* arrow, and Baruna
A snare. Indra gave her *manavedi* arrow, Ganesh
The cobra-snare and Karttikeya sweets made of nectar.
Indra gave her the *bajrabana*, *nirghantabana*,
Amritabana and *agnisara*. Marudra donated
Nidrasara, *asastamabana* and *akshaya* quiver.
Isanya gave her blue *bhujabana*, Shiva a crown
Of gems, rosary and ornaments and Ashwini Kumar
Medicine. Basuki, Takshaka and all the snakes gave
Her the cobra-snare. The planets, too, offered weapons,
Such as *madana*, *mardana*, *mohana*, etc. Brihaspati
Offered her *Dhanurveda*, *Sisuveda*, *Rigveda*, *Samaveda*,
Jajurveda and *Atharvaveda*. Arundhati
Taught her how to cook in *gauri sauri* method.
The Sun gave her *baidurya* gem; Baiswanara imparted
On her the knowledge of fire and light. Shiva gave
Lightning and *amarakosa* bow. Hemavanta
Offered her *amlan* clothes to adorn her with
And a lion to carry her. *Manapabana danda*
Was offered by Narada and a *khechari* chariot
By Ananta. Brahma gave her the swan, his carrier.
The pangolin offered her his impenetrable skin.
As her carrier, Shiva offered his bull, Vishnu

His Garuda, Indra his Airavata, Kamadeva
His lion, the Wind his deer, Baiswanara his sheep,
Yama his buffalo, Karttikeya his peacock, Baruna
His crocodile, Ganesh his mouse, the Sun his seven
Horses, the *dikpalas* a lion and Ashwini Kumar his tiger.
Kubera gave her *ratnabali* and Kamadeva *pannaga*.

O Parikshit! Offering her all their weapons
And dresses, the gods said, "Mother! We gave you
All that we had. Bless us so that our devotion
To you remain intact. Kill Mahisasura and give
Us back our heavenly abode." Durga replied,
"I'll surely wipe out the demons". She emerged
Out of the fire, in her real form.

13

Durga's Stay at Ratnagiri

'Listen, King Parikshit!
With a look that encompassed the whole creation,
Maheswari started her journey, riding a lion.
Her thousand hands with thousand weapons were
Outspread, her head touching the sky. Scared
Of her terrible figure, the gods cried out,
"Save us, Mother!" The hem of her skirt hung over
Sixty-five *yojanas* of land when she moved along.
On a mountain to the north-east of a jungle
Called Uddana, on the banks of Saraswati,
She alighted and took her seat. At its foot was
Jenabati city, to its north was a banyan tree
Called Jata and to the far north was Kulabati city.
All those places were located near the Labana sea.
The gods in heaven were watching each of her
Movements carefully. Hiding her extra hands
Inside her body and her weapons in the *khechari*
Chariot, Katyayani stayed seated where she was.
Close to Singhala island, there were five settlements,

Such as Jenabati, Chandapura, Sambhupura,
Birijapura and Chandalapura, girdled by Lakshmibhadra
And Saraswati rivers, flowing from the Meru mountain.
The whole place measured five hundred *yojanas*
And five hundred fingers, in which there was
A fruit garden with trees, such as jamun,
Coconut, mango, jackfruit, betelnut, banana,
Harida, grapes, orange, wood apple, tamarind,
Barakoli and amla. Ratnagiri nestled snugly,
Surrounded by four mountains, such as
Raktasingha, Tundagiri, Simhagiri and Vindhyagiri.'

King Parikshit interrupted, 'O sage! I'm eager
To know why the settlement was called
Chandalapura.' The sage explained:

'In Satya Yuga, Nahusa was the king
Of Sara island where it did not rain for five
Years. For the first two years, with the king's
Help, the subjects managed themselves somehow.
Still there was no rain. The king gave away all
The foodgrains he had among the subjects
Which lasted for two more years. But seeing
No hope for rain, the king held a *yajna* which
Failed to please the Rain-god. When the brahmins
Sought Basistha's advice, he said, "For disrespecting
The gods in the past, we're now subject to calamity."
However, he met Brahma and told him,
"There had been no rain in Nahusa's kingdom
For five years. Because of the benevolence
Of the king, the people could manage themselves
For four years. O Lord! People and animals are

Dying from hunger every day. Do something to save
Their lives." Hearing this, Brahma commanded
Narada, "Go and find out where paddy is available.
Since you travel across the three worlds,
You can easily trace it." Narada left for
The earth and, looking for foodgrains,
He visited the seven islands. On the banks
Of Saraswati, he met a *chandal*, Ambika by name,
Who possessed vast acres of land. The *chandal*
Informed him, "All the land you see around here
Is mine. I've stored heaps of paddy in this twelve-
Acre patch. They have been piled on planks of wood
With no cover over them. A total of five *mebakshas*
Of paddy lie here, exposed to sun, rain and cold."
Narada asked, "How long did you take to save
So much of paddy?" Ambika answered, "In Satya Yuga,
Jalandhar was the king of Singhala island. He had
A sweeper who used to collect human faeces
And dump them in my backyard. A paddy plant
Grew there which yielded three measures of paddy
Grains. Next year I sowed them in my land and got
Three *nautis*. I lent them to my neighbours on
An interest of five *gaunis* for every twenty *gaunis*
Of paddy. This way my stock of paddy increased
Phenomenally. Once, calamity befell the kingdom
Of King Jimutabahana. He borrowed from me
One lakh *bharanas* of paddy. At the time of return
I told him to pay the usual interest, not a grain
More than it. For my benevolence, people praised
Me and wished me a long life. Because of their
Blessings I outlived Satya Yuga and am still alive."

Narada said, "Listen, Ambika! There has been
No rain in Nahusa's kingdom for five years.
The subjects are going without food there.
You're the only one in the world who can save
Their lives." "Yes, I can," the *chandal* said,
"But on one condition. I've a daughter.
I don't find a suitable groom for her.
Whoever marries her would get all the paddy
As dowry." Hearing this, Narada shut his ears
And went back to Brahma. He informed him,
"O the Creator! O Narayana! O Lord
Of the world! There lives a *chandal* on the banks
Of Saraswati in Singhala island who has
A stock of five *mebakshas* of paddy. He can help
Nahusa to save his kingdom from calamity."
Brahma asked Nahusa to fetch the paddy from
The *chandal* and give it away among his subjects.
Nahusa reached the *chandal* and asked him
For the paddy. Ambika said, "You're a king
Of Soma clan. Should you force me to do
As you say? It is for you that we live in peace,
Conducting the religious activities without
Fear." "Who is forcing you to do as I say?"
Nahusa asked him. The *chandal* explained,
"I have taken an oath to offer my paddy to anyone
Who marries my daughter. Now it is up to
You to consider." Nahusa left the place
And reported to Brahma, "The *chandal*
Has enough paddy to feed my subjects for
Seven years. He asked me to marry his daughter.
Should I defile my clan by marrying a *chandal*?"

Brahma fell silent for a moment. He, then, called
Basistha and told him, "Collect the paddy from
The *chandal* somehow and give it to Nahusa."
Basistha went to Ambika again, who welcomed
The sage respectfully. The sage told him, "You're
Righteous. You know, offering food to the hungry
Is worth donating seventy-two *medhas* of gold.
If you give away your paddy, you'll live in heaven
Forever." The *chandal* replied, "I don't know you.
One who marries my daughter will get it."
Basistha returned to Brahma and told him what
The *chandal* had said. Brahma told him, "Marry
His daughter and save the creation." Basistha
Went again to the *chandal*'s house, accompanied
By Markanda, Paulasti, Agasti and many *brahmarsis*.
When he asked Ambika to present his daughter
Before them, his joy knew no bounds. He set about
Making arrangements for the marriage.
On a Sunday, the first day of the bright
Fortnight of Margasira, the marriage between
Basistha and Arundhati took place. Sage Agasti
Solemnized the marriage, tying the hands
Of the bride and the groom with holy grass. Holding
A conch filled with water and some sesame seeds
Put inside it, Ambika took the vow to give
All his paddy to the son-in-law. Then the grass-knot
Was unfastened and a fire ceremony was held.
After it was over, the groom and the bride had
A sumptuous meal, Basistha returned to heaven
With his wife and Nahusa went back
To his kingdom with the paddy.

Basistha and Arundhati lived together
As husband and wife. Under Basistha's spiritual
Influence, Arundhati's sin of being a low born
Was redeemed. Whatever she cooked tasted nice;
The *brahmarsis* and *rajarsis* appreciated it.
She helped her husband in religious activities
And was soon counted among the women of heaven
As the sixty-fourth Annapurna. In course
Of time, she gave birth to a son, Shakti who
Later became a great sage. Shakti's son was
Parasara and Parasara's son was Vyasa.
I'm one of the sixty thousand sons of Vyasa.
With our spiritual power, we redeemed the sins
Of the three worlds. Now I'm telling you about
Chandalapura. Those who ate the *chandal*'s grains
Produced more crops. Happy to see it, King Nahusa,
In the *chandal's* honour, named the settlements
As Chandalapura.'

Hearing this, Parikshit said,
'I'm happy to learn this. You dispelled my doubts.
Now I am eager to know more about Sri Durga
Who settled herself on Ratnagiri mountain.
What did she do next towards the redressal
Of the sufferings of the panicked gods?'

Glory to Narayana!
Glory to Narakeshwar!
You save mankind from hell; you're benevolent.
You pervade the whole creation; the universe
Is illumined with your radiance. For being
Your devotee, Prahlad was tortured by

His father Hiranyakashyapu. You laid
The wicked demon on your knees and tore him
Apart. The deluge cannot harm you; your *maya*
Is unknown even to the gods. How can an ignorant
Man, as I am, explain your greatness?
Your body measures ten thousand *yojanas*.
Your finger-nail is big enough to contain
All the living beings. You killed Hiranya
And ordained Prahlad as Indra. You relieved
The gods of oppression and agony. Seeing
Your incarnation as Narasimha, the gods
Were scared. They sent Lakshmi to propitiate
You. Seeing your beloved, your anger
Pacified. You changed into a *yogi's* figure
And looked calm and peaceful. May my mind
Be focused on Narasimha. May I have
Salvation with his blessings.

O Noble ones! Worship Narasimha
And get rid of all health hazards. It'll settle
Your disputes and make you live longer.
You'll be blessed with children and nectar
Will shower on you. You'll have salvation;
Your sins will be atoned; you'll succeed
In life and lead a pious life.

May I serve at Narasimha's feet
All my life, says Sudramuni Sarala Das.

14

Mahisasura Informed of Durga's Arrival

'Listen, O Parikshit!
Seated on the summit of Ratnagiri,
Durga cast an ominous look on Jenabati,
That caused disturbances in the city of the demons.
It was the ninth day of the dark fortnight of Ashwin.
When Chanda and Munda, the two brothers, had been
To the forest on hunting. While looking for the prey,
And when it became midday and they
Went into the river to have a bath.
While bathing, their eyes alighted on some golden
Lotuses floating by. Half-bathed, they went
In the direction from where they were coming.
To their surprise, they found a woman sitting
On the mountain, golden lotuses tumbling down
From her feet. Presuming that she was no other than
Goddess Lakshmi, they wondered why Narayana
Had turned her out of his abode. A woman
Of matchless beauty, she was sitting there silently,

A veil over her head and eyes downcast.
Going near her, Chandasura asked, "Where
Do you come from? Who is your husband?
Whose daughter are you? You're so young
And beautiful. What did you do that provoked
Your husband to forsake you? Are you
A demoness or a supernatural being or a dweller
Of the forest? Mahisasura's kingdom, of course,
Is quite safe, but this forest is teemed with
Wicked demons and wild animals who might
Devour you after the sunset. We're in charge
Of the forest; it is our responsibility to see
That no untoward incident takes place here.
What led you to abandon your family? If you
Agree to be our wife, we'll offer you plenty
Of wealth and ornaments and love you more
Than our lives. We'll serve you as faithfully
As we can and sacrifice everything to make
You happy. We're the commanders of Mahisasura
Who is the monarch of the three worlds."
When they stopped, Maheswari, with a smile
On her lips, gave them a sidelong look that bowled
Them over. They stood agape, putting a finger
On their mouths. She told them softly, "O demons!
Here are the answers to your queries.
My mother is Fire and my father Anakara.
As the daughter of Fire, I'm of Nirakara's clan.
My husband's name is God, the Almighty.
I'm ill-mannered and intolerant. I'm not loyal
To my husband as I'm not cut out for conjugal
Relationship. In the very first night, I refused
To sleep with him. In anger, he turned me

Out of the house. For my deviant behaviour,
I failed to lead a family life and was forced
To come here for a shelter. When I've given up
The hope of my life, should I fear the wicked demons?"
Her words caused a panic in the demons; they
Drew aside, realizing that it was impossible
To get her. Collecting himself, Chandasura asked
Her, "Do you agree to be Mahisasura's queen?
If you do, we'll inform our king about it."
Durga replied, "Tell him that I've come here
Only for him." Hearing this, they shut their ears,
And told her apologetically, "You're our Goddess.
We feel sorry for all that we told you at the start.
We beg pardon of you." So saying, they left.

Chanting "Shiva!" Chanda and Munda
Proceeded to Mahisasura at a speed
Faster than the wind. By the time they reached
The destination, Mahisasura had already
Adorned the throne after his meal. Seeing them,
Mahisasura asked what brought them there.
To which they said, "O Lord! You're omnipotent.
Today we went to the forest to hunt. While
Bathing in the river, we saw golden lotuses float by.
In our attempt to find out where they were coming
From, we reached a woman sitting on the summit
Of Ratnagiri. Her dense, curly hair had the beauty
Of a cloud; her forehead shone like molten gold;
Her beautiful roving eyes and her sidelong look
Could rock a mountain; her nose, as bright as gold,
Could enchant an onlooker and her drooping
Earrings glinted in the light of the sun. O Lord!

Her feet were like lotus-leaf, as red as ruby;
Her lips like *jaba* flowers; teeth like diamond
That shone like the moon; her voice like that of cuckoo
In Spring; her words could hypnotize sages;
Her throat more beautiful than *kunda* flowers;
Her dangling arms like stems of water lily;
Her chest as life-giving as that of Suravi;
The sight of her breast, like Rahu swallowing
The moon, swallows the race of men and when
Clothes are removed from it, they look like the sun
And the moon. O Lord! The dark forest was lighted
By her radiance. Her slender waist supported
Her wide chest. She can change the seasons
By the power of touch. When she takes someone
Into her arms, summer feels colder than
The sandalwood paste. Her embrace changes
The rainy season into summer. O Lord!
The touch of her breasts fills her paramour with
The nectar of the autumn dew. The touch of her arms
Makes one feel warm in winter. The one whom
She takes into her lap feels the mirth of spring
In him. Her breasts and hips are full and her
Deep navel is captivating. The stem of a lotus
Plant cannot pass between her breasts; it seems
Kamadeva would concede defeat to her in war.
O Lord! Between her breasts runs a line
Of dark hair, looking like a blue line between
Rows of gems. Her thighs are like inverted
Banana trees. Her gait is as attractive as that
Of a swan. The soles of her feet look like
The *ashoka* flowers, the toes like *champak* buds
And toenails like the *tarata* flowers. When

She moves, lotuses bloom at every step. Her face
Looks like the rising moon. The moon on the full
Moon day will fall short of comparison as
It has stains on it. She has doe-like eyes,
Sweet smiles; she is calm and generous.
She comes of a noble family; she is righteous
And well versed in scriptures. It is a delight
To see her; she is smart and capable.
She is a Vaishnavi, virtuous and noble.
She is hundred times more beautiful than
Rambha. O Lord! Prajapati, putting aside
His duties, invested all his time and energy in
Making her. Her chest is lovely, breasts lovelier.
O Lord! She earnestly desires to have you.
She asked us to send you to her. You're of a noble
Family, so is she. It seems both of you are
Made for each other."

O Parikshit! Hearing her being so praised
By Chanda and Munda, Mahisasura was drowned
In the sea of lust. Kapilasingha's son left the throne
And held them in deep embrace. He took off his gem
Necklaces and put them around their necks. He told
Them, "You're truly my friends. I implore you
To fetch her. Why didn't one of you stay with
Her? In your absence, someone, seduced by her
Beauty, might take her away! O Friends!
I feel like dying for her! Fetch the gem of that
Woman to me." He asked them to leave with
A golden palanquin, studded with diamond
And elaborately decorated, one lakh chariots,
Five lakh horses, three lakh foot soldiers, a group
Of musicians and plenty of jewellery for her.

There was celebration all over the kingdom,
With golden flags atop houses, spraying of sandalwood
Paste on the roads, women waiting with plates with
Flowers and lamps, burning of camphor dust
And sprinkling water mixed with camphor and musk
At every doorstep, canopies hung with clusters
Of gems and pearls and all temples decorated.

Chanda and Munda, with the troops,
Marched on through the forest until they reached
Ratnagiri. The air was cool and sweet-smelling.
They found her sitting where she was, her radiance
Illumining one thousand *yojanas*. Placing the jewellery
Before her, they said respectfully, "We did as you
Said. Hearing about you, the king's joy knew no
Bounds. He has sent these jewellery for you.
O mother! The glory of a woman lies in having
A husband in her youth, and you're going to achieve
It. The king has agreed to make you his wife. Now
Put on these ornaments and adorn the palanquin.
Let's proceed to the king. Good times have come
In your life. Be merciful to us, O Bhabani!"
Durga replied, "How can I marry someone whom
I haven't seen even for once? How can I believe
You? You've to take some more pains to go back
To your king and tell him to come to me. I will
Like to go with him. But how can it happen
Unless we see each other? We need to know
Each other before taking a decision. You're
Telling me lies, considering that I'm
A woman and can easily be duped. Now
Go back and persuade your king to meet me."'

15

The Killing of Chanda and Munda

'Listen, O Parikshit!
Chanda and Munda returned to Mahisasura
As quickly as they could. Seeing them,
Mahisasura, felt immense joy.
They informed him, "O King of kings!
That Vaishnavi refused to believe a word
Of what we said. She asks you to visit her.
If she finds you deserving, she'll accompany
You to your palace in a ceremonial procession."
Mahisasura flared up, "She can never be
A pious woman. A woman, so curious to know
About a man other than her husband, must be
A real flirt. Panic sweeps the three worlds
When I move out. How does a common woman,
Such as she is, dare test my merit? O Chanda
And Munda! Rush to her immediately. If
She agrees to come with you, it's so far so good.
If not, bring her here forcibly."

Chanda and Munda departed post-haste.
Brandishing their weapons. The sky resonated
With their war cry; the earth rocked under
The weight of their feet. Reaching Ratnagiri,
They told her, "O Mahatmani! Your message
Infuriated the king, who ordered us to fetch
You forthwith. If you don't obey his order,
We'll take you forcibly, pulling you by the hair."
Durga replied, "I abide by a code of ethics.
As great kshatriyas, you should understand it.
Who to complain if the sea crosses the shore?
What will the subjects do if the king becomes
Unfair to them? How can one help if the cloud
Refuses to rain or the trees do not produce
Fruits or men behave with women?" Biting
Their lips in anger, the demons said, "We don't
Know what you mean by ethics. But, to us,
It means devouring the sages, men and hermits
And drinking wine. We don't know
Where you came from; now you will be
Finished off for your own ego." Durga
Warned them, "You stupid demons! You'll dig
Your own grave if you violate the laws
Of God. Don't underestimate me. I'm
The slayer of demons." Infuriated
By her hurtful words, they swore loudly
And stretched their hands to catch her.
Letting out a roar of rage, she gave them
An angry stare that sent them sprawling
Onto the ground with a loud noise.
Next she produced Chhaya and Maya
Out of her, who had a single body that

Pervaded the three worlds. Her lips touched
The sky and her tongue the netherworld.
She was Kalaratri; she had eight hands with
Weapons in them. Durga commanded her,
"Hurry up! Enjoy yourself feasting on
The flesh of the demons."

Like a hawk, she swooped on the demons
That caught them unawares. Frightened
By her gigantic figure, they took to their heels.
She went on striking them with the cutlass that
Left many of them dead. Excited by the sight
Of blood, Kalaratri ate a bellyful of their flesh
And drank their blood to her heart's content.
She did not even spare the elephants, horses
And the workers who had accompanied the troops.
She turned around and rained down arrows
On the demons. Her mouth hanging open,
She swallowed many of them. Unable to counter
The attack, the demons scattered away like birds
Without a nest. She stretched her hands
For many *yojanas* and picked each of them.
Not a soul had survived to pass on the news
To their king.

O Parikshit! At the palace, Mahisasura
Was waiting for Chanda and Munda to return,
Not knowing that they had been gulped by
Kalaratri.'

Glory to Katyayani, Foe to the demons,
Whose abode is Ratnagiri.

Glory to goddesses Chhaya and Maya,
Destroyers of Chanda and Munda!
Sudramuni Sarala Das seeks refuge
At their feet.

16

The Killing of Shumbha and Nishumbha

Shuka told King Parikshit:
'You heard about Sri Durga's astonishing
Feat. This is one of the examples
Of her countless heroic exploits, which
No one can express in words.
King Mahisasura's only thought now was
How to get the woman whom Chanda
And Munda had mentioned. His intense desire
For her love made him restless. A mood
Of melancholy descended on him. When he thought
Of her, he felt a touch of Spring air in him.
The day passed, so did the night. As soon as
It became morning, he hurried to meet
Shumbha and Nishumbha.

Looking sick and broken down,
He could not utter a word. Sorry to see
His condition, Shumbha and Nishumbha took

Him in their arms and asked him the cause
Of his grief. Mahisasura stated, "Look!
Chanda and Munda told me about a woman
They had met on Ratnagiri. She was as beautiful
As she was virtuous. On my orders they went
To Ratnagiri to fetch her. The day passed, so did
The night, but they didn't return. I'm afraid
They might have been killed by her. I was too
Worried to have a wink of sleep last night."
Shumbha and Nishumbha told him, "O King!
Have you lost your mind? Those inclined to
Others' wives, suffer most. You're the Lord
Of the universe, God of gods. What makes you
Think a mere woman has killed them? Please
Retire to your palace and have some rest.
We're going there to find out the truth." Sending
Him away, they left for Ratnagiri, accompanied
By their army. Looking as huge as the Mandara
Mountain, they proceeded with unwieldy maces
In their hands. They wondered: Where did
The woman come from? Surely, the king's days
Are numbered, otherwise, why would he send
Us to look for the woman? How disgraceful
It is for warriors, such as we are, who have
Conquered the three worlds! Have the demons
Fallen from grace?

Jenabati city was one hundred eight
Yojanas from Ratnagiri. Now as Durga's eyes
Fell on Jenabati, the porch of the palace near
The Lion Gates crumbled into dust. A small
Fire started in the kitchen and spread everywhere,

Burning down Mahisasura's palace.
With no clouds in the sky, it rained heavily,
Damaging houses and villages severely.
A vulture, sitting on the throne went on eating
The flesh of the dead, turning its face northwards.
From the roof of the queen's abode, the hooting
Of an owl was heard. Meteors rained down on
The city, and the yelping of the jackals was deafening,
Things were missing from where they were.

While passing through the forest, Shumbha
And Nishumbha could not trace Chanda
And Munda and their soldiers. Katyayani had left
No clue; she had swallowed them completely
And had drunk every drop of their blood.
The song of cukoos and the pleasant forest air
Delighted them. Reaching Ratnagiri, they saw Durga
Sitting on it. Stunned by her beauty, they were surprised
To see her all alone. Without fear and shame, they
Quickly got onto the mountain. She was well dressed
And adorned with precious ornaments. Disguising
Themselves as her admirers, they stood before her.
The slayer of demons did neither raise her face
To look at them, nor did she speak a word.
Shumbha and Nishumbha asked her, "O Goddess!
Where do you come from?" She replied,
"I was born in the Meru mountain. I didn't have
The luck to have a family of my own. Abandoned
By my husband and turned out of his house, I've
Come here. I chose this place so that the beasts
And demons could easily see me and eat me up.
Intolerant by nature, I couldn't cope with anyone
In my life." The demons asked, "Chanda and Munda

Had come to you with the king's message. Why did you
Deceive a great king such as Mahisasura?" Durga
Replied, "There can be no sin greater than falsehood.
With respect to the divine law, the sea doesn't cross
Its shore. Had Mahisasura really loved me, he would
Have come to me in person. Isn't it embarrassing
On my part to visit someone I don't know and tell
Him about my virtues in the presence of others?
I don't know the names of those you just mentioned.
They were discourteous and shameless people.
While they came forward to take me forcibly,
As if by a miracle, their heads fell off their
Bodies. God punishes those who do not follow
The ways of truth. You seem to be kind, learned
And benevolent. I'm happy to see you and hear
Your words. Now let me know your whereabouts."
They said, "O Maheswari! You're the jewel among
Women. Our scriptures say a virtuous woman,
A benevolent God, a noble man and a pious
Brahmin are spiritually superior to others.
We are the sons of King Mahidas and the grandsons
Of Tadakasuara. We're mightier than Indra, but
Scared of Vishnu in all our births. We started
Meditating on Brahma at the place where river
Ganga meets the ocean, living on only air.
It continued for nine thousand years during
Which our bodies melted away many times,
And formed again, our nails, faces, noses and legs
Growing anew.

At the end of nine lakh years of unflinching
Devotion, Brahma appeared, seated on a swan.
He wished to offer a boon to us. We begged him,

'Grant us the boon that no man will ever kill us.
We know how Krishna, the incarnation of Vishnu,
Destroyed the demons.' Brahma cautioned us,
'Vishnu is a trickster; he can take the form of a man
As well as a woman. Demon Bailochana was not
Killed by any man. To kill him, Vishnu was born
To him as his daughter, Malati. Therefore, I bless
You that no man or woman can kill you.'"

Durga, feigning innocence, told them, "That
You'll live for a long long time, I fear, you'll have
Many wives besides me." Shumbha and Nishumbha
Replied, "Listen! We asked Brahma to tell us the secret
Of our death. Don't let it on to anyone. We disclose
It to you as we love each other. He said we would
Die when we put our hands on each other's head.
We're the rulers of Singhala island. We've conquered
Heaven. It's on our might that Mahisasura has
Become the monarch of the three worlds. We defeated
Baruna and robbed Kubera of all the wealth.
Brahma, Vishnu and Maheswar can never be our
Equals. If you really love us, come with us to our
Kingdom." Durga told them, "I'm touched by
Your sweet words. I was looking for Mahisasura,
But after meeting you, I forgot all about him.
I've abandoned my relatives. I've decided to be
Your wife. I've no desire for wealth and riches,
But I've terrible weakness for dance and music."
Delighted, Shumbha and Nishumbha told her,
"We're skilled in all forms of dance and music.
We'll perform the *tandaba* dance to please you."

Overwhelmed by emotion, they danced
As best as they could, Durga clapping and cheering
Them from time to time. She was saying, "It's my
Good luck that I met you and enjoyed your dance.
You're the Lord of my life. I've sacrificed everything
For you. I'm greatly impressed by your performance;
Now put your hands on each other's head."
With the passion of lust inflaming in them,
They forgot the note of caution Brahma had
Sounded out. Carried away by her sweet words,
They did as she said, oblivious of their ensuing
Death. Those whom no one in the three worlds could
Slay, were now lying lifeless, because of their lust.
Seeing Shumbha and Nishumbha dead, thirty-three
Crores of gods arrived there, leaving their heavenly
Abode. Happy and relieved, they said in chorus,
"You've relieved us of our agony. You're
The Saviour of the three worlds."
The most powerful commanders of Mahisasura,
Such as Chanda, Munda, Shumbha and Nishumbha
Were killed by misusing Brahma's boon. People
Rejoiced at the news of their death.

O Noble Ones! Think on Durga.
May she remove all your impediments.
Take refuge at her feet. May your devotion
To her reflect in your thought, speech and action.
With her one thousand hands and one thousand
Weapons, she will destroy the wicked and protect
The righteous. Chanting her name saves you
From the fear of death, removes all your

Obstacles, protects you from misfortune, removes
Your sorrows, saves you from fatal diseases,
Instils wisdom in you, grants you a long life,
Bestows on you Lakshmi's blessings, blesses
You with children if you have none and
Saves you from danger. She fulfils the wishes
Of sages and wise men who meditate on her.
You can please her by listening to her story
Or by chanting her name.

I'm narrating to you the *Vishnu Purana*
Which is the essence of *Sri Bhagavata*.
I bow to her day and night, says Sarala Das,
Praying for the well-being of mankind.

17

The Killing of Chamara and Bemala

Shuka said, 'O King!
You're listening to the story of Durga's heroic
Exploits, how she outwitted the demons,
The conquerors of the three worlds
That ultimately brought about their death.
O the Wise! Know that seducing others' wives shortens
One's lifetime.' Brimming with hope, King Parikshit
Said, 'May I be liberated from my earthly life by
Listening to her story. Tell me, how King Mahisasura
Responded to the news of his commanders' death.'
Shuka replied:

'Waiting anxiously for Shumbha and Nishumbha
To return with the woman, Mahisasura was painting
A rosy picture of his union with her. Sitting
On a coral platform outside the door, he was
Spying on the street restlessly, when Kala
And Bikala reached him on their return from

Vindhyagiri. They told him, "O Lord! For your
Greed for a woman, you've gambled away
Most of your valuable assets. First, Chanda
And Munda went to her with their soldiers,
All of whom were brutally slain. Next you
Sent Shumbha and Nishumbha who, lured by
Her into singing and dancing, laid down their
Lives." Shocked at the news, Mahisasura cried out,
"No, I don't believe it. How can anyone kill
Them whom the gods daren't challenge?"
Kala and Bikala explained, "O Lord! That woman
Is a she-devil; she has eliminated all your
Men by fraud and guile." Plunged into despair,
Mahisasura sent for Chamara and Bemala.
When they came, he commanded them, "Leave
With one thousand soldiers forthwith, collect
Information about Chanda, Munda, Shumbha
And Nishumbha and collect the details of
That woman, her character and conduct.
Have you ever heard of such a woman in your
Life? I've been here since Satya Yuga, but
Never did I come across a witch of a woman
As she is!" He ordained them as his commanders
And instructed them, "Fetch her by pulling her
Hair." Without delay, Chamara and Bemala,
Accompanied by one thousand warriors,
Marched on. Reaching the Uddan forest, they
Surrounded Ratnagiri, on the summit of which,
Durga was seen sitting, her head bent down.
They went to her and asked, "Where do you
Come from? Chanda, Munda, Shumbha
And Nishumbha came to you; they never

Returned." Durga told them, "This is the way
Of the world. Here, no one lives forever. All
Pass away, leaving their virtues and vices
Behind. They returned to where they had come
From. Human life is like a bubble; it stays
For a while and then disappears. Is there
Anyone immortal in this world? No one knows
Whether you'll die today or tomorrow. You're
Aware of Brahma's boon to Mahisasura.
But that Brahma is also subject to death."
Chamara and Bemala warned her, "Stop your
Rhetoric! Do you agree to marry Mahisasura
Or not? If you do, we'll take you to him with
Greatest care and respect. If you don't,
We offer our willingness to marry you."
She said, "I've been wishing to marry him since
Long. I won't marry anyone other than him.
Listen, I've two daughters who are as beautiful
As they are virtuous. I would like to offer them
To you." She called out to her daughters, Chhaya
And Maya, sounding out to them that she had
Arranged suitable grooms for them. The girls
Came out, seductively dressed and with a crowd
Of ornaments on them, their buns decorated
With flowers of many colours. Bewitched by
Their beauty, the demons thought they could
Entice the whole world even without ornaments.
Introducing them to Chamara and Bemala,
She said, "These are my daughters, Chhaya
And Maya. I leave them in your care." The joy
Of the demons knew no bounds, they left
The place with their brides.

They took them to Namagiri, a hill
On the banks of Lakshmibhadra, where their
Troops had been stationed. They spent the day
In merriment, in drinking, having a lot of fun
And cracking jokes. When it became night
And the warriors fell asleep, the demons wished
To make love to them. They were heavily drunk,
And their minds had gone blank. Taking
Advantage of it, Chhaya and Maya mounted
On them, and pretending to have sex with them,
Tore their chests apart. With a roar of rage,
They launched a sudden attack on the warriors
And killed all of them, except Kala and Bikala,
Who were wise enough to duck into a cave.'

18

The Killing of Kantimala, Raktabirjya, Biraghanta, Kaladanda and Bidulaksha

'Returning to Jenabati city, Kala and Bikala
Told Mahisasura about all that happened
The night before:

"As instructed by you, Chamara and Bemala
Met the young woman on the summit of Ratnagiri.
Captivated by her beauty they begged her for
Her love, to which she replied, 'Hearing about
Mahisasura's great achievements, I decided
To marry him. The king's wife is like your mother.
How dare you treat her otherwise!' O Lord!
She offered her two daughters to them who killed
Them at night on the Namagiri hill fraudulently.
In the morning, we found them lying dead, their
Faces upwards and their hearts torn apart.
The warriors who had accompanied them were also

Killed. Shumbha and Nishumbha had made
The same mistake and had to pay the price."

Hearing this, Mahisasura broke down in
Grief. A sense of guilt seized him.
He mumbled, "My dear ones! I sent you to do
My work, it's for me you laid down your lives.
I've become the monarch of the three worlds
Because of your sacrifice. Now that you're
Gone, it bears heavily on me." Saying so, he rolled
On the ground in bitter agony, and a while
Later, he got up, hissing like a snake.
Being informed, the rest of his commanders,
Such as Raktabirjya, Biraghanta, Kantimala
And Bidulaksha assembled there. Looking
At them, Mahisasura said, "You're the only
Ones I'm left with. I command you to go
To Ratnagiri at once and bring that stupid
Woman, pulling her by the hair. She has killed all
My men by deceitful means. See that you carry
Her in the air, not letting her feet
Touch the ground. I'll mince her flesh,
Cook it with her blood and eat it." Raktabirjya
Told him, "What you say is right. It makes
My hackles rise. O Lord! The four of us
Are your most loved ones. When we punish
Someone, we don't discriminate
Between a demon and a god. The earth cracks
When we walk, and the gods shake in fear.
Do we care that wicked woman who is an
Outsider? But there is a problem. If we kill
A woman, it will be a sin. If we don't,

It'll be like submitting ourselves to her.
Now, tell us what to do." Kala and Bikala
Interrupted, "'Don't take her so lightly because
She is a woman. She is the one who killed Chanda
And Munda mercilessly; she is instrumental
For the death of Shumbha and Nishumbha.
She slew Chamara and Bemala in the same way
As Narasimha did to Hiranya. Do you still
Say she is a mere woman? She is an enchantress,
Skilled in warfare. So, be careful and take with
You as many warriors as you can."
Kantimala roared out, "Whoever she may be,
Who cares? I'll bring her here presently." So
Saying, he jolted out of his seat, brandishing
His iron mace. Seeing his fury, Raktabirjya,
Biraghanta and Bidulaksha got themselves
Ready to go. With a large army, they set out
For Ratnagiri. The earth seemed to give way;
The gods in heaven including Brahma were
Scared. Reaching their destination
Towards the end of the night, they surrounded
Ratnagiri and raised a war cry that deafened
The three worlds, while the Goddess was watching
Their activities from the summit of the mountain.
They challenged her, "Where would you hide now?
We'll finish you off now and here."

Filled with inexplicable anger,
She wiped the sweat that was pouring off
Her forehead. From the sweat that dropped
Onto the ground, Narayani was born.
She was blue-complexioned, her face as white

As a lotus. She had conch, wheel, mace and lotus
In her four hands. Adorned with crown,
Earrings and necklaces, she looked radiant
And seemed to be in the world of her own.
Durga let out a roar of rage, from which
Baseli was born. One of her legs was on the earth,
The other one touching the sky. She wore her hair
Loose. She was of red complexion with
A lusty look. She had a *konta* in her right hand
And a silver cutlass in her left. Durga, then,
Gave an angry stare at the demons, from which
Bhairabi appeared. She had one leg and four
Hands; straggly hair, and she carried weapons,
Such as trident, *dambaru*, *khatwang* and bow.
She was white in complexion; her body glittered
Like coral. Durga breathed out noisily;
Brahmayani was born from her nose. She was
Of *kumkum*-complexion, with eight hands,
Four heads and two legs. She had the *ajagaba*
Bow, sword, cutlass and rosary in her hands.
Next, Durga raised her hands and gave a loud
Cry. Indrayani appeared from the tip of her sword.
She was adorned with a crown of gems on
Her head and *baijayanti* necklace around
Her neck. She carried thunder and the *ardrabali*
Bow as her weapons. She was as fast-moving
As Uccaihsraba. She had one leg, two
Heads and one thousand hands. She was as
Radiant as fire. Durga let out a wild cry,
From which Dakeswari was born. Maheswari
Was born from Durga's navel, who had five
Faces, three eyes on her forehead, two legs

And ten hands, a bright gem hung from her
Neck. She was as white as *kunda* and camphor.
She was armed with the *pinaka* bow, arrow,
Parshurama's axe, sword, *phala*, shield,
Thunder, mace, the *kodanda* and trident.
From Durga's navel, Chandrakanta was also
Born, looking terrible. Jogeswari was born from
Her throat, Kamala from her cheeks, Tripuramohini
From her eyes, Katyayani from her cheeks
And Bhadrakali from her arms. Bikakali
Was born from her belly, armed with a spade
And a snare. She was of dark complexion,
Squint-eyed, curved body and a wagging
Tongue, sticking out. Her forehead was
Daubed with vermilion; she was gigantic in size,
Her head touching the sky. From Durga's arms
Chandika was born. She had three heads,
Three hands and three legs, Ugratara
From her navel. From the soil scratched
By her feet Tarini was born. She had one leg,
Four heads, four hands and a slender waist with
A lion as her carrier.

O Parikshit! Sixty-four *yoginis* were born from
Durga's body, each more radiant than the other.
Durga herself was born on a Tuesday, the eighth
Day of the bright fortnight of Ashwin. She took
Many forms to wipe out the demons.
Glory to Maheswari who descended on the earth
With *yoginis*. Glory to Katyayani who is always
Drunk and busy slaying the demons. O Goddess!
You liberate mankind from the bondage of space

And time. You're a comet to the demons
And protector of the righteous. Your ways are
Inscrutable, unknown to the gods.
Glory to the sixty-four *yoginis* whom
I pray day and night. O Bikarali! O Kankali!
O Betali! You're skinny with a garland
Of heads around your neck. You're armed with
Sword and cutlass. Your body is smeared with
Blood. You're Ramachandi. You're Brahmayani,
Seated on Garuda. You're Indrayani riding
A cobra, you're Rudrayani moving on a bull,
Bhairabi riding a vulture, Bhadrakali
Seated on a tiger, Ugratara on an ox,
Mahamaya on a lion, Biraja on a tiger,
Chamunda on a bear, Kankali on a peacock,
Samarasti on a camel, Matangi on a donkey,
Mahamaya on a deer, Barahi on a dog, Bikarali
On a cloud, Behati on a sheep, Chandrakanti
On a goat, Kamakshi on a monkey, Tarakshi
On a bahutia, Betali on a cat, Chanchala on
A buffalo and Katyayani on an elk.
You sing and dance wildly. You're
As calm as you're angry. You're
As innocent as you're ferocious.
O Parikshit! This is the story
Of the sixty-four *yoginis*.'

Sudramuni Sarala Das says:
O Noble ones! I'm unlearned and impious.
I've been a farmer from an early age. I'm ignorant
Of scriptures. My wisdom falls short
Of gratifying the curiosity of the wise men.

The *Vishnu Purana* is as unfathomable as
An ocean. Vishnu's mercy is as uncountable
As the sands of the shore. Narmada Saraswati,
Krupajal's daughter, is worshipped
As Sarala Chandi in Kali Yuga.
She is Goddess Hingula. She is also Mangala
As she is the liberator of the souls of mankind.
Oh! How can I measure the depth of the ocean,
Being ignorant of the ways of devotion
And the rules of worship? It's my fortune
To have a glimpse of the Goddess who tells me
What to write. O Learned ones! Forgive me for
My mistakes. Listening to Hari's story is as virtuous
As offering horse-sacrifice to God. For the well-being
Of mankind I'm narrating the *Chandi Purana*.
I'm poet Sarala Das, the devotee of Sarala Chandi
Of Jankherpur. One who listens to the *purana*
Will be saved from misfortune. O Learned ones!
I told you the story of the sixty-four *yoginis*;
By listening to it, you'll be blessed with
A long life, wealth, children and salvation.

x x x

Shuka continued, 'Listen, Parikshit,
To the names of the sixty-four *yoginis*.
They are as follows:

Chhaya, Maya, Narayani, Brahmayani,
Rudrayani, Bhairabi, Indrayani, Maheswari,
Baseli, Ugratara, Tarini, Chachika, Ambika,
Khechari, Bhagabati, Bilasuni, Kamala, Shanti,
Katyayani, Madhabi, Chamunda, Anandi,

Mahanandi, Sarupa, Barahi, Ferunda, Nagari,
Keshari, Bhuchari, Karali, Betali, Bhadrakali,
Kankali, Kalika, Pitasuni, Bhalunki, Kankamukhi,
Sampadi, Samudi, Mekhali, Anuchhaya,
Mahabali, Gopali, Mohini, Kamaseni,
Kamarupi, Kamakshi, Chandi, Chaturayani,
Kubhadrayani, Kapali, Rudra, Shyama, Gauri,
Bhadrakshi, Dakeswari, Nimanjai, Urdhanetra,
Bimala, Nirmali, Pingalaswari, Siddhangi,
Poelani and Sureswari.

Fond of living on the bones, skin and flesh
Of men and animals, their eyes fell on
The gathering of a huge number of demons.
Their tongues, outstretched, wagged violently
At the sight of food in front of them. Faint
With hunger, they appealed to Durga,
"You gave birth to all of us, but how
Can we survive if you don't give us food?"

Pointing at the demon soldiers, Durga told
Them, "Go and eat these demons. Share it among
Yourselves. Let there be no leftover; consume
Their bones, skin, flesh – everything. Don't
Complain that it was not enough. You will
Have much more very shortly." With great
Joy, the starving *yoginis* swooped on the demons
Like a hawk. They swallowed whoever came
Their way, including elephants and horses.
Each chose her own prey and ate him up.
The demons retaliated with all their strength,
Using *konta*, mace and arrows. But the *yoginis*

Dodged every attack by making themselves
Invisible. Their sudden disappearance
And reappearance confused the demons; in fury,
They poured down the arrows like the rain
In Shravana. The *yoginis* gulped down the arrows
Effortlessly. Behaving as enchantresses,
They duped the demons into being killed.
During the course of the battle, Bidulaksha
And Bhagabati confronted each other. Bewitched
By her beauty, Bidulaksha threw away
His weapons and begged her, "O moon-faced one!
I'm drowned in the sea of your beauty. Save me."
Bhagabati tricked him into going with her
To the arbour, shaded by *madhabi* creepers, on
The banks of Lakshmibhadra. They walked along
Like man and wife, hand in hand. Reaching
There, they sat together and had a lot of fun
That excited Bidulaksha's lustful desire.
She took him into her lap, kissed him on his cheeks,
And while drawing him closer to her heart,
Bit his head into two halves. Another bite
At his chest tore his body into shreds.
The earth heaved a sigh of relief. A great
Rejoice went up in heaven. His fellow commanders
Kantimala, Raktabirjya and Biraghanta
Could not get wind of it.

After killing Bidulaksha, she went back
To the demons. To her delight, she found
The *yogini* sisters busy destroying the enemy.
Kaladanda, the king of the netherworld,
Was battling with Baseli, firing five

Arrows at a time at her, which Baseli crushed
With her five fingers. Then, he shot
Eighteen arrows, which broke into pieces
As soon as they hit her. Next, he sent
Sixty-four arrows, all of which she caught with
Her left hand. Then, he fired one hundred
Twenty arrows, and then, one thousand arrows
At her. The twangs of the bowstring deafened
The world. Baseli let out a roar, so
Terrible that Kaladanda's bow, quiver,
Mace and sword were burnt down.
Completely disarmed, he landed a blow
On her chest; the sky resonated with the sound it
Produced. The hand that could crush a mountain
To dust, began to bleed. In return, Baseli knocked
Him out with a severe blow on his chest. She,
Then, struck him with a sword that broke
Into pieces. Next, she hit him with her
Cutlass, which, too, fell into pieces. Then, she
Wrestled with him, tore his heart apart, but,
Still he did not succumb to the injury.
She wrung his neck, but it was of no avail.
When all her attempts failed, she realized that
He was invincible. Exhausted, she fell silent.
Just then, she heard Yama's voice coming
Through the air: "O mother! He is out of
The clutches of death; so he is named Kaladanda.
Fire cannot burn him. But if you leave him
As such, he'll continue to trouble us."

Realizing the agony of the gods, she
Pounced on his chest and made him her

Carrier. Riding on him, she entered the battlefield.
Finding Kaladanda vanquished, Yama prayed
To her with greatest respect.'

Glory to Abhaya, who rides a lion,
Red in complexion, whose face is daubed with
Blood, who has long teeth, a curved mouth
And penetrating eyes, whose tongue is
Outstretched and wagging, who has a garland
Of heads around her neck and one of whose
Feet is on the earth and the other in the sky.
O blood-faced Goddess, clad in red silk,
Whose mouth can swallow the three worlds,
Whose beauty can overpower Kamadeva!
You're firm; you're Aparna, a foe
To the wicked. You've large lips, as red as
The *bimba* fruit, a narrow forehead
And a garland of hibiscus flowers
Around your neck. You don't discriminate
Between your devotees, whether he is
A brahmin or a *chandal*. You live on
The flesh of buffalo, sheep, goat and boar.
You bathe in blood. You look terrible
With cruel eyes and a skinny body.
Your glory is immense, says
Sudramuni Sarala Das benignly.

'O Parikshit! Those who hear
The story of Kaladanda's death are not
Summoned to Yama's abode. Scared of him,
Yama had to flee his abode; so did Kala
And Bikala. In Satya Yuga, during his reign

Of fifteen thousand years, Yama dared not
Visit his kingdom. Now that he is gone,
Yama was greatly relieved.'

O Mother! The Saviour of the gods!
Accept my prayer. Those who listen to the story
Of Kaladanda's death are liberated. I pray
At her lotus-feet, seeking her blessings.
She'll remove my sorrows, redeem my sins
And protect me from Yama's wrath.
I take refuge at the lotus-feet of Baseli,
Says Sarala Das with a basil garland
Around his neck.

x x x

Sage Shuka continued:
'The battle between the demons and the *yoginis*
Took a violent turn as Ugratara and Kantimala
Had a face-off in the battlefield. Kantimala
And his five lakh soldiers launched a severe
Attack on Ugratara, raising a battle cry that
Deafened the sky. She mused, "This Kantimala
Is a burden on the earth. He has the benefit
Of Lord Shiva's boon that no one could kill him
In war." As a suitable alternative to warfare,
She changed herself into a luscious young woman,
As radiant as the lightning. Overpowered by
Her beauty, Kantimala passed out. Regaining
His consciousness, he begged her, "Dear me!
I long for your company. Be kind to me. I fall
At your feet and earnestly ask for your love."

Ugratara told him, "I've taken a vow that I'll
Marry only him who fulfils my desire." Kantimala
Promptly replied, "I'll do as you say. O dear!
Tell me what you want." Ugratara said,
"You've to carry me on your shoulders, and, not
Caring for others' ridicule, take me to the Mandara
Mountain. Then only I can become your wife."
Promising to obey her, he said, "Come, sit on
My shoulders." She asked him to wait until
Sunset to avoid public attention. When the sun
Went down, Kantimala carried her on his
Shoulders and walked on. When they reached
Behind the Vindhyagiri mountain, to the south
Of Lakshmibhadra river, near Kulabati Patna,
She said, "It aches me to sit on you so long;
Let me stand on your shoulders for a while."
Kantimala suggested, "If you don't feel comfortable
With my shoulders, you may get onto my head."
O Learned ones! See, how far the lust for
A woman can lead a man to. It pulls him like
A rope pulling a bullock. She pressed his shoulders
With her hands with a roar. Suddenly the sky
Was flooded with her radiance and the demon
Sank into the netherworld. Seeing Kantimala
Dead, the gods rejoiced and strew flowers
On her. Thirty-three crores of gods sang
In chorus, "O Goddess! You saved us
From the hands of the wicked demon."
The battle continued as usual, Raktabirjya
Had no knowledge of Kantimala's death. Of the five
Commanders Mahisa had sent there, three were,
By then, dead. Raktabirjya and Biraghanta were

The only ones who continued to fight. Biraghanta
Was mightier than the gods; he did not count
Indra, the Moon and Shiva among his equals. Hissing
Like an angry snake, Raktabirjya, armed with
Bow, arrow and mace, challenged Narayani.
As a mountain girdled by the rainwater, he was
Surrounded by a large band of archers. He looked
As radiant as pomegranate flowers. Decked in
Flowers of multiple colours, he wore a garland,
Earrings and a waist band of hibiscus flowers.
Looking like the rising sun, he directed his chariot,
Pulled by one crore lions, to the abode of the sun.

Riding Garuda and armed with conch,
Wheel, the *gandiba* bow and mace, Narayani
Confronted Raktabirjya. As she cried out,
"Hurry up! Eat them!" the flock of bloodthirsty
Yoginis spread over the whole sky. Some of them
Chased the demons, ululating loudly. Some had
Smeared holy ashes on their foreheads; others
Had tied a piece of cloth around their necks
And worn loin-clothes. With tridents and cutlasses
In their hands, they swooped on the demons like
A cast of hawks. They swallowed thousands of arrows
Fired at them and withstood the strike of the maces.
Disarming the demons completely, Maheswari
Landed blows on the demons that sprawled them
Onto the ground, upturned. Then Barahi pounced
On them, tore their hearts apart and drank
Their blood. Then, she caught some more by
The hair, spinned them in the air and consumed
Mouthfuls of their flesh. The *yoginis* beat

Many demons with maces, pulling out their hearts
With their teeth. In fear, the demons began
To flee, but the *yoginis* caught them from behind
And bit off their flesh. Their cry "Catch them!
Kill them!" filled the air. Like the birds who
Had lost their nests, the demon soldiers
Scattered around in a state of confusion.

A fierce battle ensued between Raktabirjya
And Narayani, each shooting arrows at
The other. Raktabirjya tried all kinds of arrows
On her, such as iron arrow, *parbata* arrow,
Rudra arrow and *bajrasuchi* arrow, all of which
Were either blocked or destroyed by Narayani
In the midway. With her *tikshnamuna* arrow
She destroyed his bow. The demon, then, drew
His sword and struck at her. Making herself
Invisible, she destroyed his sword with thunder.
In anger, the demon took his mace and struck
At Garuda, who fell unconscious. Seeing that
Narayani had lost her carrier, Durga sent her
A lion to ride on. Riding the lion, she hit him
With her cutlass that broke his mace in half.
Another strike with the cutlass chopped off
His head into two parts. Like two mountains,
They fell from the sky with a deafening noise.
A great cheer went up from the gods in heaven,
Who showered praises on her.'

I bow to you, O Narayani! You've no
Beginning, nor end. You're the incarnation
Of Brahma and Vishnu, the slayer of Raktabirjya

And the destroyer of the demons. You're Kankali,
Betali and Dakeswari. You're dressed in
Red silk with a garland of heads around your
Neck. Your face looks like the moon; you're
Mohini. Brahma is unable to describe your
Glory. How can a human being, such as I'm,
Do it? You're the Saviour; you're Sarala Chandi
Of Jankherpur, says Sarala Das.

Hearing from Shuka the news of the battle,
Parikshit said, 'O sage! I feel blessed to learn
About Durga's heroic feats. Tell me, what followed
Thereafter.' Shuka said, 'Listening to it, your sins
Will be redeemed. Wherever Raktabirjya's blood
Fell, thousands of Raktabirjyas were born from
There. Wherever you look around the battlefield
Of five *yojanas*, you'll find Raktabirjya everywhere.
Each of them was armed with *konta*, sword, mace,
Spade and hammer. The battlefield resonated
With their war cry. From the summit of Ratnagiri
Durga called out to the *yoginis*, "Chase them!
Kill them!" At which the sixty-four *yoginis*
Knifed into the crowd of Raktabirjyas, killing
Them and eating up their flesh and bones.
But, from their blood that fell to the ground,
Thousands of Raktabirjyas showed up.
The gods from heaven warned the *yoginis*,
"It's from his blood that thousands are born.
Don't let their heads fall to the ground."
Realizing that it was too hard a task for them,
To do, Durga produced one lakh *dakinis* from
Her body. She commanded them, "Lie on the ground

And suck every drop of blood that falls from
The demon's body." The *dakinis* did as she said
And sucked the blood, collecting them with
The help of their cutlasses. For three days
The battle continued; still Raktabirjya
Could not be eliminated.

Extremely worried, Durga shook her
Sword from which Kalika appeared.
Her hands were upraised, hair tousled
And complexion dark. She hid herself inside
Narayani's cutlass and devoured the entrails
Of each demon killed by Narayani. Chamunda,
Kalika, Kali, Betali, Maheswari, Mahamaya, Dakeswari
And Bhadrakali gobbled down the demons, like
Rahu swallowing the moon, sticking out his
Tongue. Grabbing ten to twenty demons at a time,
They broke their hands and gnawed them piece
By piece to satisfy their infinite hunger.
The fierce-looking *dakinis* revelled in killing
And consuming the flesh, bones and blood
Of the demons. It was a ghastly sight to see someone
Swallowing a demon, his head sticking out of
Her mouth. Someone had swallowed the legs
Of the demon while his hands were hanging from
Her mouth. Another was gnawing at the ribs
Of a demon. Someone had wrung a demon's neck
And tucked him under her arm.'

O Noble ones! The *yoginis* changed their
Form from time to time. How far can I go with
The details? I'm not able to narrate every bit

Of what Katyayani had told me. That's as vast
As the ocean. The more you say, the more is
Left unsaid. Listening to Chandika's story
Redeems your sins. It bestows on you all that
You crave for: righteousness, wealth, joy,
Salvation and children. Sarala Das sings
Her glory wth great devotion.

'O Parikshit! Those who read this scripture,
The pangs of old age and sickness do not touch
Them. You feel as if nectar is showered on you.'

x x x

Learning from Shuka that the battle remained
Inconclusive for three days, Parikshit said, 'Never
In my life had I heard of such things happening.
Who did Raktabirjya worship? How could he turn
To thousands after being killed? O Vyasa's son!
Pray, tell me what does the scripture say about it.'
At this, Parasara's son meditated on Vyasa for
A while, who bestowed on him the power to see
The past and the future. Then, he explained:

'It was the beginning of Satya Yuga, says
Vishnu Purana, when the demons, scared of Vishnu,
Used to please Shiva and Brahma by their devotion.
For nine thousand years, Raktabirjya worshipped
Brahma who offered him a boon. Raktabirjya
Begged him, "Grant me the boon that I won't be killed
By Vishnu's wheel or thunder or any other weapon
Of the gods. Fire won't burn me; water won't
Drown me, nor the curse of the gods will harm

Me. I'll be unbeaten in war in the three worlds.
I'll defeat the Moon and the Sun, and King of Death
Won't frighten me. There is one thing else,
I won't be slain by a man; if my blood
Falls on the ground, I'll rise out of it in thousands.
May my blood change into sperm from which
The likes of me will be born." As Brahma had
Vowed to fulfil his wishes, he granted him
All that he asked for. To bring about a quick
End to the battle, Durga commanded the *yoginis*
And *dakinis* to pounce on Raktabirjya one by
One. During his fight with Narayani, aided by
Yoginis and *dakinis*, Raktabirjya was slain.
O Parikshit! Those who hear the story of his
Death are not subject to Yama's anger.

Seeing Raktabirjya dead, Biraghanta
Rushed to Narayani, seeking revenge. Narayani
Called out "Kill him!" At this, the *yoginis* and *dakinis*
Surrounded the demons, a hundred of them for
Each demon. The bodies of the demons, as stiff
As thunder, turned soft when Narayani's
Forces touched them. The *dakinis* swallowed
Many of the demons; the more they ate, the hungrier
They became. They had their faces daubed with
Vermilion and their outstretched tongues
Kept wagging for the blood of the demons. Scared,
Many demons left the battlefield, leaving Biraghanta
Behind, who was still battling hard. Narayani
Commanded Bhadrakali, "Now it is your turn
To take over." Accompanied by Chamunda, Chachika,
Ambika, Ugratara, Kankali and Betali, Bhadrakali

Surrounded the enemy. Biraghanta and his soldiers
Put up a brave fight, shooting lakhs of arrows
At Bhadrakali who foiled their attack successfully.

Bhadrakali charged at Biraghanta
And knocked the camel he was riding down
To the ground. Leaving his carrier, Biraghanta
Hurried to his chariot, from where he fired
Five thousand arrows at a time at Bhadrakali.
Tripura managed to stop them while Chamunda
Struck his chariot with her sword so forcefully
That it fell into pieces. As Biraghanta fell down,
The sixty-four *yoginis* surrounded him.
Tripura held his left arm, Ugratara the right,
Baseli held his waist and Bhadrakali
Pulled out pieces of flesh from his body with
Her teeth. The two Chandis pulled out his arms;
They took away his head and legs and hurled
His torso at the demon soldiers who fell many
Yojanas away. A great warrior, such as
Biraghanta, who was mightier than Indra,
Lost the battle and fell dead at last. The demons
Who survived began to flee, but the *yoginis*
Caught them from behind and finished them off.

Kala and Bikala, Mahisa's messengers,
Escaped from their hideouts in the mountain
And left for Jenabati in a hurry. Reaching there,
They informed Mahisasura, "O Lord!
All of your commanders such as Raktabirjya,
Kantimala, Bidulaksha, Biraghanta and Kaladanda
Have lost their lives in war. There is no trace

Of their skin, flesh and bones anymore."
Awestruck, Mahisa fell from his throne, as if
He was hit by a thunderbolt. Kala raised him
To his feet and sprinkled some water on his face.
He brought him round and made him sit on
The throne. Mahisa knelt down, and, beating his brow,
Said mournfully, "We belong to Rahu's family
And Kashyap's clan. Simhika, Daksha's daughter,
Is our progenitor. We provoked the Sun and the Moon
To act against us. We were hostile to Indra as
He killed Jambu. In our attempt to occupy heaven,
We've reduced ourselves to the condition we're
In now. Proud of being immortal, we chose
The path of wickedness. Our whole clan is wiped out
As we incurred Narayana's displeasure. Brahma
Gave me his word that I won't be slain by Vishnu,
Brahma, Indra and the Sun, that the deluge won't
Destroy me, and that none in the three worlds will
Defeat me. All my devotions to him have come
To a naught." Mahisa told this in the assembly
Of his courtiers. Andhaka, his minister, told him,
With folded hands, "You gambled away all your
Assets in the process. The gods tricked you into
Losing everything. The woman you took into
Confidence deceived you outright.
You reaped what you had sown."'

19

The Tale of Bailochana

Sage Shuka said, 'Andhaka was telling
Mahisasura, "Long ago there was a king named
Bailochana who was as powerful as he was
Boastful. He sat in meditation for three
Thousand years, praying to Brahma who,
Pleased with his devotion, granted him a boon
That he would be immortal, that he won't die
From snakebite, Yama can't take his life,
Nor water can drown him to death, that
Neither Vishnu's wheel nor Shiva's weapons can
Pierce into his body and that he won't be slain
By man. Scared of him, the gods took shelter
In the waters of the sea and prayed to Vishnu
To save them. To relieve the gods of their agony,
Vishnu changed himself into a young woman
Of matchless beauty, naming himself as
Malati. Malati lived in the Nilandi forest,
To which Bailochana would come on hunting.

On a Sunday, the thirteenth day
Of the bright fortnight of Phalguna, Bailochana
Met Malati while travelling through the forest.
Could a man ever ignore the seductions
Of a woman who was as beautiful as she was?
Enchanted by her beauty, Bailochana fell
In love with her. Oblivious of his power
And position, he started burning in the flames
Of lust. O Lord! You were in the same situation
As he was. Chanda and Munda, driven by
Their sexual desire, not only got themselves
Killed, but also brought death upon those who
Accompanied them. O Lord! It seems you don't
Learn anything from it. Great warriors, such as
Sumbha and Nishumbha did the same mistake
And lost their lives."

Mahisasura interrupted, "Tell me,
What happened to Bailochana and Malati after
They met each other." Andhaka resumed,
"In all ages, men have been deceived by women.
Seeing Bailochana completely overpowered by
The passion of love, she asked him to take
A vow if he wanted to have her. Bailochana
Vowed to marry her and abandon the wives
He had already had. His state of mind during
Those times was too difficult to be explained.
At the time, I was his minister. One day he
Came to me with the girl; he told me how her
Beauty had overwhelmed him. I was sorry
To see the emperor of nine islands not

A bit interested in the affairs of his kingdom.
I was asked to see to that, which I did. The love
Between them grew with years. In course
Of time she became pregnant. The king took
All steps to make her happy. It was a time
Of great rejoicing in the kingdom. He performed
All the rites, as was the custom, with austerity.
It went on like this for nine months. On
The eleventh day of the bright fortnight of Jyeshtha,
The king took Malati into his lap and expressed
His desire to go hunting for a day.
Malati said, 'Your absence for a moment bears
Heavily on me. I'll be waiting for you without
Food until you return.'

Listen, Mahisasura! Her innocence
And loyalty was a complete sham; her real
Intention was to find ways and means to kill
Him. She asked, 'How will I know if there is
A threat to your life in the forest?' To which
He replied, 'Brahma's boon ensures that
I'll outlive the four ages; that Brahma, Vishnu
And Maheswara won't be able to kill me.
Neither shall I be burnt by fire, nor can
A sword pierce into me. The deluge cannot
Drown me. I won't die by day, nor by night;
Not inside the house, nor outside. No man
Can kill me. Listen, dear! Brahma has planted
A brown hair on my head which is the secret
Of my death. I'll die only if a woman plucks
It out.' Hearing it, she heaved a sigh of relief.
While leaving for the forest he kissed her

On her cheeks and she bade him farewell,
Wishing him the best of luck.

Riding a horse and armed with sword, *konta*,
Bow and arrow, Bailochana set out for the forest.
Narayana, alias Malati, displayed an illusion
That made the wild animals disappear. Bailochana,
In spite of trying hard, found none to kill. In
The meantime, Narayana filled his head with lice,
Which started itching severely. Returning home,
He finished his bath and meal. After passing some
Pleasant moments with Malati, he complained
To her, 'Why does my head itch?' 'There must be
Lice in your hair,' so saying, she asked him
To wait a while. She started combing his hair with
An ivory comb. She went on picking the lice and
Killing them. Bailochana was lying with his back
Towards the house, eyes towards outside. The upper
Part of his body was lying outside and the feet
Inside the house. Malati said, 'O dear! It's
Twilight already.' But Bailochana asked her
To concentrate on killing the lice. While searching for
The lice, she located the brown hair. While
Doing it, suddenly she took her real form,
That of Narayana, her body pervading the sky.
She held the brown hair firmly with her fingers.
Bailochana, inebriated, was lying subconscious
While Malati got onto his back, pressing her feet
On his head. Letting out a roar, she pulled out
The hair with all her might. The demon, with
A howl, breathed his last.

Listen, Mahisasura! Bailochana fell
Victim to a woman's evil designs. This is
What happens to the boons given by the gods.
I'm a witness to it. Take the case of Shumbha
And Nishumbha. They were assured that
They won't die unless they put their hands on
Each other's head. That woman tricked them
Into doing it. Another example is of Raktabirjya
Who was too formidable to concede defeat to anyone.
But he lost the battle and his life as well.
Why don't the demons understand this simple
Thing that life and death follow each other,
That night comes after day and misfortune
Follows fortune?"

Mahisasura replied, "I'd never imagined
That a mere woman could be the cause of the death
Of my warriors and my present worry,
My chief concern is how to protect
Myself. I'll leave my kingdom and take shelter
In the sea." Moved by the anguished words
Of their king, the demon warriors pledged
To avenge the loss. Among them were
Jamaghanta, Kalabimochana, Kankasura,
Dhumralochana, Chandasura, Prachandasura,
Lohasura, Dhanka, Bankasura, Bhaskar,
Bajranga, Kalanala, Batasura, Meghasura,
Bakasura, Ashwamukha, Gajamukha, Srikalamukha,
And Grudhramukha. Kalabimochana prayed
To the king, "Command us, O King. We'll fetch her
Instantly." Mahisasura, broken down in grief,
Said, "What price pride and fame! Those who

Carried out my command and went there, never
Returned. I won't do the same thing again. If
You so wish, you may go on your own."
Twenty-eight commanders who were not counted
Either among gods or demons, with their
Army, set out for their destination, raising
A war cry. They looked like a moving sea. Riding
Elephants, horses and lions and armed with
Swords, *lankia* and *konta*, they marched along.
The earth resonated with their angry cry.
Sahasrasira was leading from the front;
He had two thousand heads and an equal
Number of hands, his body glittering like
The Subarnakuta mountain. He had a bow in
Each of his hands; the twangs of his bows deafened
The three worlds. The column of soldiers covered
Five *yojanas* of land, all of whom were drunken
And terrible-looking. Reaching Ratnagiri, they
Surrounded the mountain raising a great din.

From the summit of the mountain
Narayani was watching the movement of the demons.
At the time all the yoginis were drinking and dancing.
The demons could hear their noise of revelry clearly.
Climbing up the mountain, Sahasrasira went over
And asked her, "O strange woman. Where have you
Come from? You killed all our commanders
By deceiving them." With a smile, she said,
"No one in the world stays forever. Those who
Are born, must die. That Brahma who promised
You immortality dies every one crore years.
The life of Shiva, the greatest of all *yogis*,

Comes to an end every one thousand
And seventy-two years. Likewise,
The period of Indra's life is one *padma*
Years. And, so also, the *dikpalas* die and a new
Set of them is born. Therefore, to think that
You'll never die is nothing but stupidity.
Why do you blame me unnecessarily? All of us
Who have come to this world are destined to die.
He who offered you the boon, has told a lie.
You've already lived long, now it's time for
You to die." Hearing this, Kalabimochana
Warned her, "If all of us are to die, why should
You be allowed to live? Woman is the symbol
Of deceit and wickedness. Had we come here
Earlier, you would have seen how powerful
We are. Considering you a mere woman,
We left you unhurt. And that allowed you
To display your evil designs." She said,
"Listen, O foes of the gods! We are not the kind
Of women you think us to be. As mothers,
We bring you to the earth; as wives, we
Spend nights with you; as Kalika, we kill you;
And as fire, we burn you after you die.
You've beginning and end, but we're the middle.
We create and we destroy. Your evil doings
Quicken the process of your death. We represent
The eternal motherhood, we're *yoginis*, the
Symbols of purity. Our ways are inscrutable.
Now, Narayani of Kali Yuga will devour
All of you." Riled up, Kalabimochana
Commanded his army to mount an attack on her.

O Parikshit! In response to the commander's
Call, the demons climbed up the mountain.
Kalabimochana had seventy crore soldiers,
Dhumralochana had fifty crores; Bakasura
One *padma*; Dhankasura three *padmas*;
Bhogasura one *padma*; Udeka seven lakhs;
Prachandasura one *mebaksha*; Chamara Danda
Three *padmas*; Chandalia ninety crores; Bajranga
Nine *sagaras*; Utpata, Mahisasura's grandson
Five *sagaras*; Samudrasura, the king's uncle,
Three *sagaras*; Mahisasura's twenty-one *sagaras*;
Jalamanthana one *padma*; Dengasura five *padmas*;
Bengasura nine *sagaras*; Kankasura fifty crores;
And Kodasura had fifty crores soldiers.
They launched an all-out attack on Narayani.'

20

The Demon Commanders Challenge Durga

Sage Shuka continued:
'Listen, O King! Besides Kalabimochana, there
Were many other commanders in Mahisasura's
Army, each of them controlling his own troops.
Seated on Ratnagiri, Durga was watching
Sahasrasira's troops who had occupied the space
Of sixty-five *yojanas* between Lakshmibhadra
And Saraswati rivers. Terrified by the sight
Of the demon forces, the gods left their heavenly
Abode and took shelter behind the south peak
Of the Malayagiri mountain. They whispered
Among themselves, "When thirty-three crores
Of gods fled their abode in fear, how is it that
The *yoginis* are least afraid of them?" Brahma
Told them, "The Goddess is powerful enough
To destroy all of them in a moment." Indra advised
Them, "Have patience. You'll see many interesting
Things happening today."'

Curious, Parikshit asked the sage,
'What did Durga do when she saw the demons
Besieging the mountain?' To which Shuka replied,
'Her face was flushed with anger to see this.
In addition to the sixty-four *yoginis* she already
Had, she produced many more goddesses from
Her body: Four *padmas* of Brahmayani, each with
Eight hands and armed with the *ajagaba* bow
And arrow; one *padma* of Rudrayani with
Mace, halberd, *konta*, arrow and sword;
Fifty-six crores of Narayani with four hands
And armed with *gandiba* bow, *kaumudi* mace
And riding Garuda; sixty-four crores
Of Indrayani, each having eight hands,
Carrying bow, arrow and snare and Airavata
As carrier; fourteen crores of Bhairabi, each
With one leg, four hands, three eyes on her
Forehead with the *kodanda* bow, lance, halberd
And *dambaru* in her hands, clad in white
And riding a bullock; nine crores of Barahi
Having one hundred heads and two hundred
Hands, terrible-looking, with weapons,
Such as spade, axe and dagger and adorned
With gem earrings; five hundred of Jala
Devi, decked in jewels and armed with
A snare; nine crores of Katyayani, their
Hair loosened and tongue wagging; fifty
Crores of Kothari; nine crores of *dakinis*;
Five *sagaras* of *pichasunis* under the command
Of Ugratara; three *sagaras* of Kankali,
Commanded by Baseli; seven *padmas*
Of Mekhali, controlled by Bhadrakali; ninety

Crores of Mahakhela commanded by Hingula;
Nine *sagaras* of Chandis with the body
Of cobra; three *sagaras* with dog's body;
Boar-faced and elephant-faced Chandis, their
Faces daubed with vermilion having Jambuswari
As their commander; fierce-looking Chandis
With human body, commanded by Chhaya;
One *padma* of Pingalakshi with the face of a swine;
Three *padmas* of Chandis riding tigers with
Chachika as their commander; one *padma*
Of Chandis with the face of a bear, ruled by
Bikarali; hundred crores of lion-riding
Chandis commanded by Mahamaya; nine *padmas*
Of Chandis commanded by Kumari; nine lakhs
Of Dakeswari under the command of Chandika;
Nine lakh Chandis, cat-faced, controlled by Pingalakshi;
And one hundred lakhs of Chandis, their faces like
That of a crow, looked after by Biraja. Besides,
There were goddesses, such as Ananta, Bijaya,
Jateswari, Ketuka, Dakshini, Uttarai, Maha
Barahi and Patalabasini.'

The list of the goddesses is too long to be
Cited fully. Bowing at their feet, Sudramuni
Sarala Das seeks their blessings.

x x x

Sage Shuka continued:
'Listen, O King! From Durga's body so many
Goddesses were born. As soon as they were born,
They begged Durga for food to eat. Pointing at
The demon soldiers, Durga told them, "Here is

Your food. Share it among yourselves Don't
Worry if you find it not enough; there's more
In store for you." As she finished, they swept
The sky and the four mountains. Their hair
Dishevelled and tongues outstretched, they
Swooped on the demons like hawks, with daggers
And cutlasses in their hands. The sixty-four
Yoginis, too, jumped from the mountain
And joined them. Each of them was assigned
A specific task, to take on a particular
Commander and his troops, kill them and eat
Them up: Narayani for Kalabimochana; Baseli
For Sahasrasira; Ugratara for Bhaskar;
Tripura for Pingalasura and Manasura;
Kothari for Satamukha; Maruchi for Jamaghanta;
Maruti for Jayasingha; Bhairabi for Kapilasingha;
Bhagabati for Jagasura; Pingalakshi for Mahisira;
Chachika for Yojanabahu; Chhaya for Bakasura;
Kalika for Parbatasura; and Polama for
Jatasura. Durga told them, "Keeping in mind
The number of the demons, I've produced so many
Goddesses. They may fall short of your
Need as you can consume mountains and seas."

Assignments completed, the *yoginis* swooped
On the demons who retaliated, striking them with
Maces that fell into pieces as they touched the *yoginis*'
Bodies. With no weapons to fight with, they fell
Victims to the *yoginis* who ate them up. But
There was no sign of a let-up in their aggression.
One demon killed, hundreds would come up.
The arrows they fired at the *yoginis* came as

The rain from the sky. The exchange of arrows
Hid the sun from view. All their weapons, such
As arrows, *konta*, maces and crowbars were
Crushed to dust. The *yoginis* treated them as if
They were a herd of goats, tossing them into the air
And swallowing them as they fell. Eighty lakh
Warriors of Dhankasura were consumed by
Kothari alone. The *yoginis* revelled in drinking,
Dancing, running around and singing. The place
Was upbeat with the noise of ululation
And *dambaru*. They devoured whatever came
Their way – elephants, horses and chariots. Having
Lost his troops, Dhankasura fought with the *yoginis*
With his unwieldy mace, but the mace, as huge as
A mountain, was crushed to powder. Dhankasura
Rushed forward to swallow the *yoginis*, but Polama
And Marakama pulled his feet apart that ripped
Him in half. Then, they began to chew a part
Each. Seeing Dhankasura dead, Brahma showered
Praises on Kothari and prayed to her, "Glory
To Kothari who is also known as Katakshi,
Matangi, Kamakshi, Kamaseni and Mohini!
You've done a great service to us by slaying
The wicked demon."'

O Noble ones! How can a feeble man,
Such as I am, describe her, to whom Brahma
Says his prayers? I take refuge at Sri Kothari's
Feet, says Sarala Das with a basil garland
Around his neck.

x x x

Shuka continued:
'I told you about the glorious deeds of Kothari
Whom Brahma had named Mohini. She relieved
The sages and hermits of Dhankasura's oppression.
After his death, they resumed their spiritual activities
Without fear and interference.

The fall of Dhankasura provoked
Triambikasura to challenge the *yoginis*. His head
Touched the sky, his body occupied the space
Between the earth and the sky that made the sun
Invisible. Seeing him, Durga exclaimed, "What
A boastful demon, showing off his might before
Me! O Marakama! Kill him!" Marakama, armed
With mace, club, bow, quiver and cutlass, rushed
Towards him, riding a wild elephant. She expanded
Herself to the size of the demon and attacked him with
The mace. But, before it could hit him, he caught
It with his left hand and dealt her with a blow;
The mountains rocked with the noise it created.
Marakama's body was too strong to be harmed by it.
His attempt to hit her again also failed. Then, he shot at
Her a fire arrow which caused fire as it reached
Her, but it was put out on its own. Then, he struck
Her with a pair of unwieldy maces that were turned
To dust by the Goddess. His maces broken, he picked
A *konta* and a club and went on beating her
Several times which proved to be of no use.
The battle continued until late into night,
The demons showing no sign of retreat. When
All his weapons were exhausted, he stood like
A burnt-out mountain. It was then that she

Struck her sword at his chest. It struck
The ground before him that made him fall down
On his back. Markama pounced on his chest
And pushed her jaws into it and tore it apart.
Then, she devoured his flesh, skin, bones and blood.
For killing Triambikasura, she was called Triambika.
With the demon gone, the earth heaved a sigh
Of relief and she felt happy and satisfied.'

Sudramuni Sarala Das prays at her feet
Day in and day out, seeking her blessings.

x x x

'Triambikasura had sixty-five thousand
Warriors, each mightier than the other.
They went on attacking Marakama with halberd,
Spade and mace. From the summit of Vindhyagiri
Mahamaya was watching how three *koshas*
Of land was soaked with blood. She jumped from
The mountain with an open mouth that covered
The earth and the sky. She swallowed the demons
In large numbers, like the earth soaking
The rain. The demons and all their weapons
Went into her belly. She devoured their flesh,
Bones and entrails; not even a drop of blood
Was left over.

O Parikshit! Who is able to narrate
The battle of Chandis in words? Bajranga
And Bhaskar, accompanied by fifteen *sagaras*
Of warriors appeared in the battlefield.
O King! As the sea stops at the shore, they

Stood before the *yoginis* as long as seven
Mandara mountains. Seeing the demons in
High spirits, Durga produced Jayachandi
And Ramachandi from her throat. She asked
The seven sisters, namely, Vindhyasuni,
Kumari, Maruchi, Amarai, Chamai, Chinai,
Kapadai and Bipulai to proceed and finish off
The warriors of Bajranga and Bhaskar.
The seven sisters, thirsty for blood, spread over
The whole battlefield. Listen, O King, to the glorious
Acts of Jayachandi who turned to sixty young
Women. With their sidelong looks and lovely
Postures, they seduced the demons into leaving
Their weapons and carriers and falling in
Love with them. Making friends with the demons,
They hooked their arms around them and plucked
Out their eyes with their fingernails. Tossing
Them into the air, they caught them with their mouths
As they fell. On the pretext of kissing, they chewed
Their heads. Tearing the demons apart, they shared
Their flesh among themselves. In a moment,
One lakh demons perished and were eaten up;
Still the *yoginis*' hunger was as before. It seemed
Like a battle between cranes and hawks.
Jayachandi was such a Goddess that after drinking
A sea of blood, she remained as thirsty.

Without having to fight, Jayachandi,
Bewitching the demons by her beauty,
Left them burning in the flames of lust.
Taking this opportunity,
She called out to Barahi, Balai, Tarai, Jarai,

Rankai, Shamalai, Dulanai, Amarai, Harai,
Kamai, Bimalai, Banai and Chachikai.
She commanded them to attack them and eat them
Up. They flew into the sky, and, accompanied by
Ugratara, Marakama, Bhairabi, Baseli, Ambika,
Kothari and Chamunda, fought with the demons
With battleaxe, dagger, cutlass and sword.
There were twenty-eight Chandis to battle
With twenty-eight demon commanders.
Their bodies were smeared with blood and face
With vermilion. Among the sounds of *changu*,
Ghumra, *mridanga* and *damandi*, the inebriated
Chandis danced wildly. Unafraid of the demons,
They caused heavy casualties in a short time.
Ugratara alone swallowed one lakh warriors.
They devoured so many of them,
Still their hunger was not satisfied.
They contained twenty-five kinds of fire in them;
Whatever they ate, it was burnt down instantly.

Seeing their warriors being slain
In large numbers, Bajranga and Bhaskar
Rained down arrows on Jayachandi
And Ramachandi. Ramachandi battled
With Bajranga and Jayachandi took on
Bhaskara, while the rest of the *yoginis*
Created panic among their warriors. Ramachandi
Shot an arrow at Bajranga that pierced
Into his heart. As he fell on his back,
She pounced on his chest and killed him.
He had worshipped Brahma for nine thousand years
And was granted the boon that his body would be

As strong as thunder, and that no weapon would
Pierce it. It was to be decimated, therefore, by
Chandi's superior power. The gods were pleased
To see Bajranga put to death and they praised
Her with love and respect.'

Glory to Ramachandi, the harbinger of peace
And happiness! Chanting her name removes all
Obstacles in one's life. She is Remover of sorrows
And the Protector of her devotees from Yama's wrath.
She rewards them with wealth and children.
O Noble ones! Your devotion to her will fulfil
All your wishes.

Thus says Sarala Das.

x x x

'Listen, Parikshit!' said Sage Shuka,
'Ramachandi's glory is too great to be put in
Words. As the battle between Jayachandi and Bhaskar
Ensued, the sun went down. Bhaskar tried on
Her all kinds of weapons, such as mace, hammer,
Konta, crowbar and sword. But none of them
Could cause damage to her body. He took the bow
And fired arrows at her; the twangs of his bow
Deafened the world. But it was in vain. Then,
With a pair of wieldy iron maces, he hammered
Jayachandi, who returned it with the strike
Of another couple of maces of the same size.
The collision of four maces gave out a loud
Clank and sparked, lighting the whole battlefield.
When the weapons broke and fell into pieces,

Bhaskar cocked his sword; his feet on the earth
And head touching the sky. Terrified by
His huge shape, the gods sent her the Pushpak
Chariot. Offering her some jewellery, Matali
Told her, "Mother! Save the gods from the wicked
Demon who doesn't allow them to enter heaven.
Let me tell you about his past life.
For fifteen thousand years, he worshipped
The Sun, living only on iron dust. He cut
Pieces of flesh from his body and consigned
It to the holy fire, as a part of his devotion.
Every piece of flesh he cut was replaced
By new ones at every sunrise.
He gave up the company of women, food
And sleep, and lay in the burning fire.
Pleased with his steadfast devotion,
The Sun appeared before him on a Sunday,
The full moon day of the month of Magha. When
He sprinkled some nectar on him, the demon
Rose from fire; the size of his body was
One thousand times greater than what
It was before. O Mother! When the Sun offered
Him a boon, he prayed, 'O Lord! I wish
To be named after you; I'll be known as Bhaskar
Henceforward. Make me as powerful as you are,
So that no one will be able to defeat me in the three
Worlds. I won't die by the day, nor by the night.
I'll not be killed by a man. My body will be
As strong as thunder and I'll live as long as
You exist.' 'So be it,' saying so, Sajna's consort
Left for his heavenly abode. O Mother! He'll cause
Trouble to you in many ways. I suggest to you

To remain in the sky in this flying chariot
And come down only when it is past fifty-seven
Lita in the evening. That's the appropriate moment
To kill the demon. Beware that he won't die
Either by the day or by the night." So saying, he left.
Positioning herself in the sky, she took fifty
Bows in her left hand, shooting arrows at the demon
Incessantly. On the other hand, Bhaskar's arrows
Broke into pieces as they hit her body. Desperate,
The demon charged at her with the Sun's wheel
From which no one was able to escape.
Having no other alternative, she flew down into
Water with her chariot, where
The wheel would not reach.

The gods were praising her:
"As long as the sun and the moon exist,
Jayachandi's benevolence will never lessen.
She protects her devotees from their enemies.
O warriors! Chant her name
And you'll win a victory in war.
Glory to Katyayani! Glory to Chandi! Glory to Hari,
The Remover of human sorrows and sufferings."'

Putting on a basil garland around
His neck, Sudramuni Sarala Das bows
At Jayachandi's lotus-feet.

x x x

Curious to learn more from the *Vishnu Purana*
That originated from Brahma, Parikshit asked
The sage to go on, listening to which he hoped to find

A place in Vishnu's abode. Sage Shuka continued:

'It became evening, but the battle between
Jayachandi and Bhaskar did not seem to come
To an end. Unable to see anything in the dark,
The soldiers were in confusion as to what to do.
Taking advantage of the chaos, Chandis
Caught them and ate up whoever they lay their
Hands on. It was a bedlam in the battlefield
With the noise of their revelry.
As a part of the plan to eliminate
Bhaskar, on a Tuesday, the eighth day of the bright
Fortnight of Ashwin, Nimanjai swallowed the sun
For nine days. It was during that period that Bhaskar
Was put to death. At long last the Earth heaved
A sigh of relief. With a conch in hand, she met
Durga and bowed to her in respect.

Surprised at her dismal condition, Durga asked,
"O Earth! What's the matter? Your face has
An unhealthy pallor. Your *kumkum*-complexioned
Body has turned as white as crystal. Your
Ampleness has disappeared; you look so pale
And worn out!" The Earth replied, "Mother!
The fear of Mahisa and Shumbha and Nishumbha
Has blanched me. When I see them, I hide myself
In the netherworld. This unfortunate situation
Has been continuing since Satya Yuga. It's all
Too much to take in." Durga consoled her, saying,
"Now that the demons are being killed, you needn't
Be scared of them anymore. Your unhappy days
Will come to an end very soon."

The Earth told her politely, "How can I be
Happy unless I devour Mahisa's flesh and blood?
Once that happens, I'll look ruddy again. It'll only
Be possible if you help me. When I'm in distress,
The righteous suffer from diseases. Those who
Admire me suffer, too. Those who walk on me
Hurt their feet. Everything grown on me becomes
Unwholesome. Those who take rest on me, die untimely.
Mantras and medicine fail to heal the diseases.
Quarrels rise among the relatives of a family.
Such things happen when I'm made to suffer.
People fight among themselves and kill
Each other. Animals are killed indiscriminately.
Family relationship breaks off. I live
Only on the flesh and blood of the sheep and goats
That people offer to God for their recovery
From illness. Since the time the demons got
The boons, such calamities have been taking place.
It's true that the atrocities of the demons have
Declined, but it has not ended yet."

Durga replied, "The deluge takes place at your
Command. You share the sorrows and sufferings
Of all created beings, but enjoy nothing. Tell me,
What I can do for you. I'll try my best to see you
Happy and comfortable." The Earth begged her,
"O the greatest of all *yoginis*! I've been starving
For ages. Your *yoginis* eat the demons; they don't
Even allow a drop of their blood fall on the ground.
See that they don't do it any longer. Ask them
To leave the corpses for me to feed on, so that
My strength and lustre can be restored.

O Merciful mother! Do fulfil my wishes."
When Durga advised her to watch the battle,
She said, "It's of no use. I'll be happy if I get
Enough to eat." Being assured of it, she left.

Durga called out to Narayani, Baseli
And Bhagabati and told them, "Considering
The distress of the Earth, you hold off your
Hunger for the time being. From now on,
Let she devour the demons. One who violates
My order, will turn to a *dakini*. She'll have no further
Birth and her life will rot in misery." Then,
She instructed Dakeswari, "Inform everyone
That they shall not eat the corpses any longer."
Dakeswari sounded out the message to everyone.

For a foolproof implementation of her
Order, Durga produced a number of *kshetrapalas*
From her feet, namely, Gorea, Khankhari, Ranka,
Kandia, Kamadeba, Jadua, Hanumanta, Ambika
And Bhalunka. In addition, she produced many
Others to keep an eye on the *yoginis*. They were
Jadumala, Hasanimala, Kandanimala, Ambua,
Khankara, Manika, Kalatunda, Babara, Bijaya,
Malla, Tuduka, Chamanda, Dahana, Shosana,
Sukuta and Jhanjhari. She deployed all of them
At various points of the battlefield. She instructed
Them, "Keep a watch on the *yoginis*. If you find
Anyone guilty, bring her to me." The *kshetrapalas*,
A rope of cow hide in one of their hands
And an iron club in the other, moved
To their respective places.

Being forbidden to eat, the *yoginis* became
Too weak to fight with the demons
Who showed no signs of withdrawing
From the battle. The *yoginis* and the demons were
Fighting in pairs: Chandika with Kalaketu;
Baseli with Bajraketu; Tripura with Yojanabahu;
Bhadrakali with Birabahu; Bhairabi with Subahu;
Brahmayani with Chandabahu; Indrayani
With Dhankasura; Ugratara with Lotasura;
Kothari with Gaganaghoti; Barahi with
Andharaghara; Marakama with Urddhakesha;
Bhairabi with Chandrajita; Kalika with
Ghantasura; Yamayani with Bakasura;
Kamakshi with Trijatasura; Pingalakshi
With Unmatta; Tadaki with Birabara;
Dakeswari with Ghodamukha; Ambika with
Birupaksha; Maruti with Tarakshi; Baseli
With Gajamukha; Mahamaya with Bimalasura;
Chhaya with Pingalasura; Matangi with
Lohasura; Sri Chandi with Medhasura,
Ramachandi with Angirasura; and Chamanda
With Chirasura.

O Parikshit! As the sun lay hidden in
Nimanjai's stomach, it was dark all over.
Stabanai and Dulanai, the two sisters, were
Killing the demons and eating them. Likewise,
The seven sisters, namely, Bilai, Bichhalai,
Nila, Balai, Upai, Utkalai and Mangala were
Doing the same. When it came to the notice
Of the *kshetrapala*, he rushed to them, raising
His sword. He scolded them, "May your mouths

Be burnt. You, greedy women! How dare you
Act against the Goddess's will?' Paying no heed
To his words, they went on devouring
The demons' flesh. Infuriated, the *kshetrapala*
Struck one of them with his sword. In return,
She cut-off his hands. Bleeding all over,
The *kshetrapala* went to Durga and reported,
"O Mother of the Universe! I caught the seven
Sisters red-handed while eating the demons.
They severed my hands with the chopper." Enraged,
Durga cursed them, "The seven of you will be
Dakinis. Leave the battlefield at once. You'll stay
Put on the banks of Baitarani as stone images
For four lakh years of Kali Yuga, with Patakeswar
As your husband. You'll be worshipped by
Men. They will sacrifice sheep and goats as
Offerings to you on which you will feed yourself.
Your sins will be redeemed by seeing
Krishna in form of a parrot every day."'

O Noble ones! I'm too ignorant to write
It. I'm unlearned, a tiller of land using Balarama's
Weapon. I live in a non-descript village. I have
Not read the scriptures; I'm illiterate and I live
A despicable life. On the night of the tenth day
Of the bright fortnight of Ashwin, I saw a woman
In my dream who put a basil garland around
My neck and taught me the scriptures.
All that she told me that night will take
A year for me to put on record.
That omnipotent Goddess ordained me as
A poet. O Noble ones!

She is Saraswati, the cursed daughter
Of Krupajal, who has been worshipped
At Jankherpur in Bharata as a *yogini*.
May my mind remain steadfast at Sarala
Chandi's feet. May I spend my days
In writing the scripture.

Thus says Sudramuni Sarala Das.

x x x

King Parikshit told Shuka, 'O sage!
I'm eager to learn about Chandi in details.
You said the sun lay hidden in Nimanjai's
Belly. What did thirty-three crore gods do about
It?' To gratify his curiosity, Shuka began:

'Durga is the greatest of all goddesses
In all four Ages. The *Ramayana* and the *Mahabharata*
Are flooded with the tales of war. Many wars
Were also fought between the demons and Vishnu
During the periods of his incarnation. But
None of them is equal to those of Sri Chandika.
The display of her skill and fortitude
Is the rarest of the rare, which words fail to express.

Carrying out Durga's command, the *yoginis*
Gave up feeding on the demons. In a day,
The battlefield was full of dead bodies. An
Overflowing river of blood passed through it,
Submerging Vindhyagiri, one hundred eight
Yojanas in length and two *yojanas* in circumference.
The *sal* tree atop the mountain sank under the waves

Of blood, heaps of corpses floating around it
And flocks of vultures drinking plenty of blood
Merrily. The terrain between Lakshmibhadra
And Saraswati rivers was completely inundated.
Crows and *sampadas* were pecking at the demons'
Flesh, while on flight.

In the absence of the sun, the three worlds
Were wrapped in darkness. The *yoginis* could
See the demons with their divine eyes, but it was
Too dark for the demons to distinguish between
The *yoginis* and the demons. For nine days
The sun did not rise. He, whose body is as vast
As the Meru mountain, had taken shelter in
Nimanjai's belly in a reduced form. At the time
The gods reached Durga and told her respectfully,
"It's for your blessing that we're now safe."
Durga interrupted, "You needn't be so complacent
About it. Don't forget that Mahisasura is
Still alive with a large number of his followers."
Brahma said, "The most formidable ones among
Them, such as Shumbha, Nishumbha, Bhaskar,
Have been slain by now. Chanda and Munda,
The conquerors of the three worlds,
Scared of whom, Indra had to quit his abode,
Have been destroyed. Now Nimanjai
Has to release the sun."

Hearing this, Nimanjai made her mouth
Wide open, through which the sun came out.
It became light everywhere. It surprised the gods
To see the river of blood. The Earth, extremely

Pleased, came to Durga with a conch in her hand.
Durga told her, "O Earth! You must be happy
Now. Your body is as radiant as gold
And you look nice and healthy. There is plenty
Of flesh and blood waiting for you. You can take
As much as you want. Now forget the past and be
Happy." The Earth replied, "Mother! By your grace
My hunger is satisfied. I don't need food anymore.
My former complexion has been restored.
Now feed your *yoginis* up. I'll be happy
To see them eating." Durga instructed
Narayani to communicate the news to others.

Listen, Parikshit! During the period
Of the sun's absence, a large number of demons
Were slain; their decomposed bodies were emitting
A foul smell. Calling out to the yoginis, Durga
Asked them to report on how many demons
Each of them had killed. With folded hands,
Narayani said she had killed five *kshaunis*
Soldiers of Jamaghanta; Brahmayani ninety
Thousand crore soldiers of Dhankasura;
Maheswari fifty-six crores of Kankasura;
Baseli thirty crores of Yojanabahu; Biraja
Three *sagaras* of Krutantaka; Dakeswari
One *padma*; Marakama three *sagaras*; Chandi
Seventy crores; Kalika one *sagara*; Kothari
Demons beyond count; Balama and Golama sisters
Two *kshaunis*; Ugratara one *mebaksha* soldiers
Of Subahu; Bhairabi three *brundas*; Indrakshi
Innumerable soldiers; Tripura five hundred;
Ambika nine *sagaras*; Matangi two hundred

Thirty crores; Bhagabati eighty lakhs; Maruchi
All the soldiers of Abalambana; Chamunda
Ten crores; Bhalunki countless; Kamala
One *sagara*; Barahi crores of soldiers of Jatasura;
Bhadrakali fifty crores; Betali twenty crores;
Ambika one *padma*; Kamakshi three *sagaras*;
Vindhyasuni a large number of demons;
Sankheswari four *kharbas*; Ananta one hundred
Padmas; Bijaya five *sagaras*; and Mahamaya
Innumerable demon warriors.

Besides those, there were sixty-four *yoginis*;
Nine crore Katyayani; three crore Brahmayani;
Fifty-six crore Narayani; sixty-four crore
Indrayani; one *padma* Kamarupa; sixty lakh
Barunai; fifteen *mebaksha* Chandi;
All of whom were born to Durga
And as omnipotent as she was.

The Earth told Durga, "Mother! I know
Every incident that had occurred here since
The creation. I've witnessed the wars
Of the *Ramayana* and the *Mahabharata* in
Which Vishnu had killed lakhs of demons.
But your battle is exceptional, many times
More violent than others. Pray, instruct
The *yoginis* to clear the battlefield of the bones,
Skin and flesh of the demons."

Pleased, Durga produced some more
Blood-thirsty goddesses from her feet, such as
Vindhyasuni, Ahantasuni, Jagulai, Bilasuni,

Kamasuni, Amasuni, Bamasuni, Surasuni,
Khemasuni, Jyesthasuni and Basudhyasuni.
All of them cried for food as soon as they were
Born. "Go and drink from the river of blood,"
Durga told them. Chandis, expanding
Their bodies to the size of mountains,
Began to consume the flesh and blood like
The Meru mountain swallowing Ganga when
She fell from heaven. The sixty-four *yoginis*
Drained the river of blood, sixty-four
Yojanas deep. It took them a day and a night
To make the battlefield spotlessly clean.
Then, their eyes fell on the demons, who had
Survived the trauma of war. Not scared
Of their weapons, Bilasuni, Hathiasuni
And Brahmayani finished them off in no time.

Long ago there was a demon called
Japasura whom Brahma, pleased with his
Steadfast devotion, offered a boon. The demon
Said, "I wish to spend my life in meditation
And prayers. Bless me that I attain salvation."
Brahma advised him, "Go back to your place
And start meditating on the banks of Baitarani.
Whoever tries to break your meditation,
Will be burnt into ashes when you give
Him a sidelong look, be he Hari, Hara
Or Indra." Japasura attained *Siddhi*
In Satya Yuga. In course of time, he became
The king of the earth. He married his daughter,
Radhi, to Maya. They had a son, Bajrasingha
By name. Bajrasingha's son was Kapilasingha,

Who was Mahisasura's father. Therefore,
Japasura was the great-grandfather
Of Mahisasura, and later, his commander.
He ruled South Koshala which was a land
Of five crores of demons.

O Parikshit! Japasura enjoyed
His life to the full, but his happy days came
To an end when Hastibasini killed
All his soldiers by collecting them into
A fold with her trunk-like hands.
Broken down to see his warriors dead,
Japasura lost his vigour and was unable
To lift his bow and weapons. He sat in
Meditation on Kumandala mountain,
Thinking on Brahma. While he was in
Deep contemplation, Hastibasini pulled
Him by her trunk-like hands and swallowed
Him before he could defend himself.
This is how Japasura and his twenty thousand
Strong army were slain. All the wealth and fame
Mahisasura had earned was due to Japasura's
Spiritual powers. With his fall, Mahisasura
Plunged into deep despair.

After the death of Japasura, the kingdom
Suffered many setbacks. The demons gradually
Lost their power; they became a race of weaklings.
On the other hand, there were great rejoicings
In heaven. Mahisa had already lost twenty-eight
Commanders; none of whom could escape
The clutches of twenty-eight *yoginis*. With

Crores of demons to feed on, the Earth was
Bubbling over with excitement.

Seeing Mahisa's troops completely decimated,
Kala and Bikala, who were hiding in a nearby
Mountain, rushed to Mahisasura. They told
Him, "O Lord! All your soldiers have been slain."
Hearing this, Mahisa was so shocked that
He was lost for words. The demons added,

"Twenty-eight of your commanders are
Lying prostrate." Surprised, he asked, "Lying
Prostrate? What do you mean? Who will
Capture the woman, then?" Kala spoke out,
"Your commanders are now no more." "O I'm
Gone!" so saying Mahisa, slumped onto the ground,
Unconscious. When he was brought round,
He felt like a man who had lost everything.

Heaving deep sighs, he bemoaned,
"At last Yama found access to my kingdom.
Each of my commanders was capable enough
Of conquering the three worlds on his own.
All of them had to lay down their lives
For the sake of a silly woman. I failed
To realize that the gods had played a trick
On me. O what a misfortune!" He began
To sob. Kala asked him, "Didn't you know
That no one can escape the strike of Vishnu's
Wheel?" Mahisa explained, "After long years
Of meditating on Brahma, I got the boon that
No man could kill me. Andhaka, my minister,

Laughed it off. He cautioned me that the woman
Was one of Vishnu's incarnations. I scolded
Him harshly, saying that he was a stupid
Blind man. Had I listened to him earlier,
I wouldn't have fallen into such trouble.
The woman whom I disparage so much,
Has become a thorn in my flesh. O dear!
You departed, leaving me in the lurch!
It scares me to stay here. In which sea
Shall I hide myself? What's the use of staying
Alive after I've lost the best of my warriors?"
Cursing himself, he banged his head and fell
To the ground, as if struck by a thunderbolt.

Kalabimochana replied calmly, "While on
Their mission to serve your petty interest, they got killed.
I had told you how Chanda and Munda suffered
At her hands. Not heeding my warning, you dug
Your grave with your own hands. Now it's time
You proved your might to her. Your boastfulness
Led you to command Chanda and Munda to fetch
Her by the hair. This single order predicted
The impending doom you're now experiencing.
Now, no question of going back. Let's visit her
With our troops. Depending on the situation,
We'll decide whether to fight or draw a treaty."

Consenting to it, Mahisa ordered his troops
To get ready. He called out to Dhumralochana,
The charioteer, and asked him to be in readiness.
Dhumralochana decked the chariot, capable of
entering. The sun's abode
In gems, sapphire, ruby, pearl, silver, coral

And placed urns made of eight kinds of gems
Atop it. He yoked nine thousand horses to the huge
Chariot, each adorned with precious jewels.'

Parikshit intervened, 'O Learned sage!
The chariot you just mentioned belonged to
The sun. How did it come to Mahisasura?'
Shuka replied, 'It's true the chariot belonged to
The sun in which he used to travel across
The sky. It used to take off from behind Udayagiri
Every morning with seven horses hitched to it
And driven by Aruna. It had a single wheel
Made of the wood of the *sahada* tree. The sun
Used to circle the Meru mountain every day.
To mount an attack on the sun, Rahu was chasing
Him in a flying chariot. On the full moon day
Of the month of Margasira, both met each other.
Frightened, the sun left his chariot and took
Shelter in the Milky Sea. Not finding him, Rahu
Swallowed his chariot and later, vomitted it
Out on Ratnagiri mountain. Jambu, Rahu's
Son, took it away. Killing Jambu, Indra carried
It away to his abode. When Maya, Jambu's son,
Empowered by Lord Shiva's boon, invaded
Amaravati, Indra fled in fear. The demon grabbed
All his wealth, including the chariot. Vishnu,
Incarnated as Keshaba, killed Maya and Andhaka,
His son was slain by Brahma. Andhaka's
Sons, Raksha and Bhaksha, were slain by
Krishna. Heti and Praheti, their sons,
Oppressed the sages and brahmins and attacked
Hiranyagarbhapura. In the battle that ensued

Between them and the sun, the latter conceded
Defeat to the demons. Thus the chariot was
Passed on to them. In his second incarnation,
Vishnu killed Heti and Praheti and transferred
The chariot to Yashobantipura. Bajranga
And Kalanala, their sons, defeated Yama
And took it away. Narayana killed him
And kept the chariot in the netherworld.

Kalanala's sons, Mali and Sumali, empowered
By the sun's boon, tortured the sages and brahmins,
For which Krishna slew him and offered
The chariot to Brahma. Demon Madhu, Malyabanta's
Son, with the blessing of Lord Shiva, launched
An attack on heaven, causing panic among
The gods who fled in fear. He kidnapped
Sixteen thousand *apsaras* and made a pleasure
Trip, carrying them in the chariot across the sky.
On the way, Vishnu killed Madhu and came to be
Called Madhusudana. He kept the *apsaras*
And the chariot in Barunapura. Jalataranga,
Madhu's son, receiving a boon from Lord Shiva,
Attacked Barunapura. Defeating Baruna,
He took away the chariot and Jalandhara's
Wife with him. Vishnu killed Jalataranga
And restored the chariot to heaven. Tadaka,
Jalataranga's son, invaded heaven
And the chariot came to his possession when
Indra fled in fear. Karttikeya killed Tadaka
And the brought the chariot to Alakapuri.
When Shumbha and Nishumbha occupied
Heaven, they took it away from there and presented

It to Mahisasura. O King! This is the story
Of the long journey of the chariot before
It came to be used by Mahisasura.'

Shuka's words are as indelible as letters
On the stone; the sun and the moon are
Witness to it. He is learned, noble and well versed
In scriptures. He is omnipotent. His glory
Is like the sands of Ganga, which cannot be
Counted. He is always cheerful, not interested
In worldly life.

O Goddess! Even Vyasa cannot
Put your incredible deeds into words.
Sudramuni Sarala Das prays to you
For your blessings.

21

Mahisasura Proceeds to the Battlefield

'Listen, Parikshit, to the heroic exploits
Of Durga, who fulfils all human wishes.

Thinking on Brahma, Mahisasura sat
In his chariot, and, with his followers and troops,
Set out for the battlefield. The vast column
Of the troops looked like another sea, their weapons
Flashed like meteors in the dark sky. Kalabimochana
Was leading from the front with ten thousand warriors
And nine *sagara* soldiers. At Mahisasura's right
Was Singhanada who had, besides elephants
And horses, two lakh warriors and five *marbhuta*
Soldiers. Dundubhi was at his right, leading
Four crore warriors, two *sagara* soldiers
And one crore demons; Singhamukha and Gomukha,
The two commanders, were in the rear with eight
Lakh warriors. Mahisasura himself was accompanied
By eleven crore five *marbhuta* sixty-eight lakh

Soldiers who had just returned after eleven days
Of war. Crores of attendants were at his service,
Fanning him with black *chamars* and white
Chamars, their handles studded with pearls.
Some were raising umbrellas of peacock feathers,
Others holding umbrellas with silken covers.
Three lakh eight thousand musicians were
Playing sixty-five thousand trumpets and an
Equal number of drums and five thousand
Tamakas. Three crore eight thousand warriors
Were riding bears and tigers. They were dark
In complexion, dressed in black and putting on
Armours. They looked like the clouds of Shravana.
They had waist-belts studded with gems
That looked like storks in flight against
The background of sable clouds.

They were on their march to Ratnagiri;
The earth shook under the weight of their feet.
Ambika informed Durga, "Mahisasura is
Arriving here to wage a war against us.
Hearing the news, Chandis, long starving,
Are excited with the prospect of having plenty
Of food. They're only waiting for your orders.'
The Earth, sweating all over, told the Goddess,
"Mother! I can't bear the wickedness of the demons
Any longer. This time my sorrow has been doubled.
Look, how I bleed!" Durga consoled her,
"Bear with it for a day; you'll be relieved
Of your sorrow by tomorrow." So saying,
She created from her body crores
Of goddesses, each a Mohini.'

Parikshit interrupted, 'I'm eager
To hear their names, of what complexion they
Were and how they looked like. That'll
Redeem my sins.'

Shuka said, 'Listen carefully. Narmada
Sarasvati was the first to come, next came
Sarala Chandi. The goddesses who followed
Them were as follows:

Ambika, Baulai, Shanti, Kanti, Madhabi,
Ukhulai, Dhyai, Rukhai, Rakhai, Abatarika,
Madhu, Tarali, Bikala, Jaloka, Drami, Sami,
Uttama, Palai, Biranai, Birangamali, Pingalai,
Sadai, Bidai, Kaparai, Tanai, Dhamanti,
Sumanti, Hathi, Hingalai, Jetai, Matai,
Anantai, Bijaya, Kalandi, Tulasa, Abhaya,
Andhari, Sramuki, Saria, Bipula, Ganga,
Jamuna, Mekhala, Mahakhala, Japa, Jupai,
Manani, Chandrarekha, Marua, Maarua,
Gopalika, Madanika, Sumati, Nidrabati,
Pingala, Arukha, Suradha, Mahijata, Taraki,
Debi, Abala, Priyamati, Kala, Kamala, Saenta,
Dharamai, Jamai, Dankini, Bhayankari,
Chitrapada, Garakhi, Sadarakhi, Banadebati,
Dhabali, Mauli, Kuruli, Parekha, Surasiddha,
Mahajita, Areka Darsani, Surasuri, Udaundi,
Apurna, Sanchai, Binjhai, Mahani, Sanikali,
Mukali, Dandi, Prachandi, Bikarali, Bira,
Bitakshi, Bikuchhi, Bimati, Bhanumati,
Parikshi, Dhanumati, Rebati, Girija, Singhari,
Binghari, Bhangari, Sauhala, Tanuja, Sakembari,

Bankeswari, Jajati, Malati, Basi, Subasi,
Jashobanti, Aramai, Jemai, Angirai, Amai,
Anandai, Murai, Chingarai, Binai, Bipakshi,
Indrakshi, Jalarodri, Parvati, Uma, Upama,
Basani, Malabati, Chandasuri, Birasuri,
Sunyasari and many others. They were
Of five complexions: white, yellow, red,
Dark and fair. Those who chant their names
Are blessed with salvation and all their
Fear is redeemed. These goddesses are
Enchantresses who lure the wicked into
Their destruction.'

Thus says Sudramuni Sarala Das,
The author, praying at the lotus-feet
Of these goddesses.

22

The Killing of Kalabimochana

Shuka continued:
'Listen, O King! The goddesses I just mentioned
Are protectors of mankind. Each excelling the other
In beauty, they enchant the three worlds
And create in all living beings a will to live.
They have no beginning nor end, but only the middle.
They encompass the world with *maya*, which tempts
Even sages, brahmins and hermits
Fall victims to it. They punish the proud and rob
And defeat the wicked ones. They spend their time
Merrily, in singing and dancing. They do things
At will. They play various roles in the lives of men.
As mothers they give birth to them; as wives attend
To their sexual needs in their youth; as Kalika
Take care of them when they are old, and as fire,
Cremate them when they die. They create; they destroy.

Addressing the assembly of those goddesses,
Durga said, "Look! The tyranny of the demons

Has been too excruciating for the Earth to bear with.
Now I ask you to bewitch the demons, except,
Mahisasura, by seductions and kill them."
Receiving the orders, the Vaishnavas changed themselves
Into beautiful young women and entered
The battlefield. There was a heavy gathering
Of the demon soldiers who were making an awful din.
Seeing the women with glossy appearances before
Them, their cry froze on their lips, it was like
Garuda, King of birds, falling onto the ground
Helplessly. Enchanted by their beauty, the demons
Threw away their weapons and alighted from
Their chariots. Lethally wounded by Madana's
Arrows, they cried out, "Dear oh dear! Save us!"
Lost in the ocean of lust, each of them caught
Hold of a woman of his choice. Sporting
His moustache and prancing, one of them said,
"No one can have the company of such a harlot
Unless he took a dip in Prayaga or pleased
Lord Shiva by his devotion. For this woman,
I'm ready to forsake my family and lay down
My life, if necessary."

Seeing his soldiers enticed by the women,
Mahisasura was puzzled. He thought: It is for
These women that I have lost many of my warriors.
They failed to overcome their sensual desires
And fell victims to the women who tricked them
Into killing themselves. The charms of a woman
Can reduce the mightiest to the weakest.
Her sidelong look can raise the mountain above
The ground. The charms of her eyes can make

A stone crack." Mahisa shouted at his soldiers,
"Enjoy your time with the women as best as
You can." At this, each of the demons picked
A woman and, tugging on her hands, hurried along
To the forest, hand in hand. It was spring.
They had a lot of fun there, and, when
The night came, they revelled in drinking
And making amorous advances to each other.

The Earth informed Durga, "Mother!
All have left Mahisasura except Sindhu,
Upasindhu, Kalabimochana, Kala, Bikala
And Dhumralochana. In obedience to your command,
No woman has tried to cast her spell on Mahisasura."

It became morning. The warriors did not
Return. Curious to find out the reason for their
Delay, he proceeded to the forest riding a tiger,
With a gem-studded club in hand and flanked
By his followers. At the far end of the forest,
On the south bank of Lakshmibhadra,
He discovered all his warriors lying dead,
Their bodies mutilated. Dumbstruck, he now
Realized what might have happened to them.
His head began to reel. He fell off his chariot
And passed out. When he was brought round,
He held the dead bodies dearly and bemoaned,
"How shameless I'm that I'm still alive!" He cursed
Himself and muttered, "O dear ones! How sad,
You invited trouble upon yourself! I'd never seen
Such an act of deceit in my life. Hell with me!
I'll surely kill myself by fire." Moved by the king's

Distress, Kalabimochana, boiling mad, rushed
To Durga. Seeing him, the Goddess, her face like
The Autumn moon, advanced towards him.
At the time the enchantresses reached there, each
With a lotus in her hand. Kalabimochana was
Now sure that they were the ones who killed the demons
Last night. He left his chariot and weapons
Behind and ran towards them, seeking revenge.

Kalabimochana, Trijatasura's grandson,
Hooked his arms around sixty-five of them,
And, holding them by the feet, hurled them
Southwards. All of them fell on Rakta island,
Unconscious. They were Ananta, Bijaya, Tarini,
Kamakshi, Birali, Karali, Matangi, Tarakshi,
Shama, Subama, Kalikali, Basi, Brusali, Atagni,
Maruti, Sukeshi, Sita, Saenta, Malati, Muktabeni,
Chakra, Chandrabati, Nairuta, Prasani, Mati,
Saradha, Bimalai, Krutangi, Sasthagni, Tanuai,
Tanu, Bhanu, Medha, Sumedha, Hira, Prava, Radha,
Suradha, Lalita, Sulita, Suprarekha, Sarana,
Sashimukhi, Baseli, Chandrarekha, Indrai,
Chandrai, Bindai, Bhotai, Sarua, Parua, Sadangi,
Motai, Uchhuri, Chhaladuruni, Bikatali, Bhutai,
Atutai, Kapali, Katali, etc. Then he grabbed
Athousand of them, whom of them were:
Sankuni, Sauni, Dhatakataka, Parabati, Kami,
Bhami, Bisaadaki, Utkati, Asita, Damita, Kalika,
Jalini, Satamugru, Kampi, Kamika, Adrabali,
Rekhi, Surekhi, Namami, Natakuta, Chandi,
Chamuni, Badarika, Madhabi, Sachabi, Tara,
Suta, Hara, Dekhi, Amua, Mula, Eikara, Gabanag,

Dustai, Maratanda, Biraha, Bidhata, Kalaghanta,
Prachanda, Tanuki, Januki, Priya, Kalandi, Dhama,
Saurama, Dhamsi, Kista, Mukundi, Chamari,
Maitri, Bisnubhadra, Dhumaisita, Bhadrata,
Adangi, Bimalai, Marajita, Jigna, Jaitri and Kantani.
All those fell on Shuka island. Next, he caught
Some more and threw them one lakh *kosha* away
To fall on Singhala island. Nine thousand goddesses
He spinned in air and sent them to Bilanka
Kingdom. Then, he collected another nine thousand
Chandis and hurled them northwards, who fell
In Jambu island. Some of them were: Loka,
Ambika, Poloka, Suni, Abhaye, Birupa, Hastibasini,
Nila, Matiminja, Sarupa, Brukshalsi, Kamari,
Kamakshi, Tarakshi, Baulai, Mekhala, Upala,
Kokila, Bikala, Sathi, Duchhai, Leutsi, Kamala,
Atari, Sukhari, Chakitai, Aurai, Jageni, Jageswari,
Champai, Rupai, Sananta, Binanta, Kendukai,
Rajai, Panchasini, Sitasini, Kankai, Budhai,
Pandai, Gandai, Mati, Prasana, Hingula, Kashi,
Dhabalangi, Maruchi, Pingala, Januki, Tanuki,
Jugani, Jatika, Dursarupa, Arupa, Saunika,
Katika, Parbata, Lagika, Lotasani, Abasani,
Dakeswari, Bhulunka, Khankheni, Kankani,
Satasani, Priya, Narmada, Pitasani, Madakhala,
Janita, Bhogeswari, Sumati, Chandrabati,
Ghorarupa, Bhutarai, Dakhina, Mahirupa, Sati,
Sabitri, Rati, Damati, Jagati, Sachala, Sampadi,
Bhanumati, Jita, Jarata, Kripa, Batchhala,
Sada, Alali and Haria. All those goddesses
Stayed in Jambu island and lived on human
Beings after seducing them. Thus, Kalabimochana

Threw the goddesses to the seven islands, severely
Injured. Some of them had their faces covered
With cuts and bruises; others had their bones
Broken, still others had their limbs dislocated.
Unable to move, they lay where they fell.

Mahisasura heard about all this from Kalinjan.
But that was not the end of Kalabimochana's
Actions. He captured about one thousand goddesses
And tossed them into the air randomly. They fell
In the forest and were later known as forest
Deities, bearing the name, Kamakshi. Three thousand
Goddesses he threw into water who came to be known
As water goddesses. The names of some of them were:
Malaya, Basanta, Chiregati, Tilalochana, Dumata,
Malika, Bhabisa, Madana, Gokula, Palagni, Abhuta,
Sanghita, Panthara, Madagni, Basini, Satima,
Marita, Rasita, Sataini, Trijata, Trikuta, Nagari,
Baula, Tila, Tejya, Santani and Pingala. This is
How Kalabimochana wiped out the whole lot
Of goddesses to avenge the death of the fellow demons.

When he met Mahisasura, the king greeted him
With a reward of gold and gems. Addressing him
As the saviour of his life, he said, "You're a great
Kshatriya who saved Rahu's clan from peril.
I'm the cause of my present misery. Why didn't
I ordain you as commander before? You're
The only answer to the problems of the demon
Community. It was stupid of me to let my innocent
Warriors die helplessly. Now you're the only one
On whom I rely. You've wiped out all the *yoginis*

Single-handedly. You're the greatest of all the warriors
In the five kingdoms. You're the saviour of a great
Dynasty. I ordain you the king of the netherworld
And heaven. I've just one request to make:
Get me the stupid woman." With folded hands,
Kalabimochana replied, "Be assured that she'll be
Brought to you very soon. Long live the king
Of the three worlds! If I fail to do it, I won't
Return to you alive."

With fierce determination, that demon
Proceeded to Ratnagiri to fetch the woman,
The root of all evils. He did not take the chariot,
Nor his men. The only things he carried with
Him were a pair of wieldy maces. By the time
He reached there, Goddess Durga was sitting
On the summit of Ratnagiri alone; the nine
Crores of Katayanis were deployed in the sky
To take on the demons. Like Rahu encircling
The sun, Kalabimochana's body, as huge as the Mandara
Mountain, seemed to girdle the Goddess. Brandishing
His maces and biting his lips in anger, he asked her,
"Hey, strange woman! Where do you come from?
Why do you invite your death unnecessarily?
Mahisasura is the monarch of the three worlds.
Be his wife and enjoy your life to the lees. If
You agree, I'll offer you to him. This is the only
Way to save your life." Hearing his words,
She replied with a smile, "I find you're not in
The king's favour, or else, you wouldn't
Have spoken such harsh words to me. If you can
Bring him to me, I'll believe that he trusts you."

The demon scowled at her and roared out,
"A despicable woman as you are, how dare you
Ask King Mahisasura to come to you? When
He walks, Indra, Shiva, Brahma and Hari begin
To tremble. If you don't do as I say, I'll take
You forcibly to him, the same way as Panchali
Was taken to the royal court."

Reaching the end of her patience, the Goddess
Called out "O Ugratara! O Baseli! O Narayani!"
Suddenly lakhs of Katyayanis positioned
In the sky descended on the earth, their feet
In the netherworld and heads touching the sky.
They were armed with the *kodanda*, *gandiba* and maces.
Letting out a cry "Kill! Kill!" Narayani charged at
Kalabimochana with her mace, Bhairabi with
A trident and Baseli with a cutlass. Tripura
Trapped the demon in cobra snare, Ugratara beat
Him with thunder, Narayani shot at him a *brahmasara*,
Indrayani pierced a trident into his body, Chamunda
Hit him with a mace and Marakama struck him
With a sword that chopped off his head.

O Parikshit! Three *padmas* of Chandis
Arrived there to devour the demon's flesh
And blood which was less than enough. Seeing
Kalabimochana falling dead, the gods strew gold
From the sky. They held a meeting on the Meru
Mountain after a gap of one lakh and sixty-seven
Years. There was great rejoicing in heaven, Narada
Singing songs in seven tunes and asking
The *gandharvas* to send for the spring.'

23

The Killing of Mahisasura

'Too shocked at the news of Kalabimochana's
Death at the hands of the women in the battle,
King Mahisasura fell off his throne with a thud
And passed out. Demon Dhumralochana took
Him into his lap and brought him round,
Sprinkling some water on his face. Regaining
Consciousness, the king cursed himself
And bemoaned, "What a damn shame! How I wish
I died long before! Do I live to see all these?
O my dear friend, Kalabimochana, the Rising
Moon of the full moon day in my Jenabati city!
The void left by your death can never be filled:
I guess my days are numbered. Even if
I live, how shall I rule the kingdom, having none
To assist me? O Dhumralochana, Sindhu
And Upasindhu! I advise the three of you to leave
The place and save your lives before it is too
Late. This time I'll fight single-handedly, giving up
My lust for wealth and power and fear of death.

I'd so many great warriors and wise men
Who could forsee the past and future, but
None of them spoke a word about what was
Going to happen. I defeated the gods and demons
With my might. It is my bad luck that I end up
Losing everything. No one ever hinted me
About the villainy of the gods. Being carried away
By the boastful words of my commanders,
I failed to take necessary precautions on time.
At last my fate betrayed me. All my commanders
Died before my very eyes, letting me live a shameless
Life." As a kshatriya it was all too much for
Him to take in. Between sobs, he continued,
"When all that I was proud of is lost, I don't
Mind whether I win or lose or whoever defeats me.
Infatuated with a wicked, despicable woman,
They gambled away their lives.
I had many and she had none.
How could she, a mere woman, be not afraid of
Men? Alas! Vishnu is my only adversary.
I would have been happy if he had killed me.
On the other hand, if I had defeated him, I would
Have been praised in the three worlds. Had I
Earlier wished to be killed by man, I would have
Earned the virtue of being killed by Vishnu's wheel.
Now I'm on the brink of death. I'm going to die
For no fault of mine, but because of the gods'
Conspiracy." So saying, the king of the demons
Struck the Dhabala mountain with his sword.
O Parikshit! That nine-*yojana*-long mountain,
Crumbled, cut into half, that scared the gods.
Waving his sword, he rushed to heaven, yelling,

"I'll kill all the gods today. I'll wring Brahma's
Head and spare no one." Seeing Mahisasura
Ascending the sky, the gods left their abode
And fired arrows at the sky incessantly
That formed a wall, eight thousand *yojanas*
Long and nine hundred *yojanas* thick.
Unable to penetrate into the sky, Mahisasura
Asked Andhaka, his minister, "Now that the way
To heaven is blocked, what should we do now?"
Andhaka replied, "In spite of warning you many
Times, you still keep saying that she is a woman.
You don't believe her to be the incarnation
Of Vishnu. Don't you see she is holding conch,
Wheel, mace and the *gandiba* bow in her
Hands." Mahisasura looked at her and was
Surprised to notice the signs of Vishnu on her.

When the day was done, he retuned
From the sky. After ablutions, he meditated
On his father and changed himself into
A buffalo, of the size of a mountain.
At the time Durga and the *yoginis* were passing
Their time in revelry, all of them inebriated.
The mighty demon, disguised as a buffalo,
Began uprooting Ratnagiri mountain
With his horns. One hundred *yojanas* of it
Was inside the earth. It was two *yojanas* long
And two hundred *yojanas* and five hundred
Fingers high. He held Ratnagiri on his horns
After uprooting it, on which seven *padmas*
Fifteen *mebaksha* crores of *yoginis* were
Frolicking. Panicked, Marakama, informed

Durga, "Mahisasura has arrived here in
The darkness." All the goddesses raised a cry
When Mahisasura hurled Ratnagiri nine
Thousand *yojanas* away, to a place called
Marahattaka on the borders of the Skanda forest,
In south Saurastra.'

Glory to Katyayani, the greatest of *yoginis*,
Who feeds on flesh and liquor, the Protector
Of mankind, the Remover of obstacles,
The Destroyer of the wicked, the Well-wisher
Of the three worlds and the Saviour of the world.
How can I narrate your glory who Brahma
Worships? I bow to her hundreds and thousands
Of times, says Sudramuni Sarala Das
With greatest respect.

x x x

'Listen, O King, to the *Vishnu Purana*
To know more about what happened next.

By the time Mahisasura uprooted Ratnagiri
And threw it away, it was midnight already.
Dhrumalochana told him, "Let's go back.
It is not desirable to stay on at the place
You've just conquered." Appreciating what
Mahidas's grandson had said, the king of the demons
Journeyed back to the palace. After his bath
And meal, he retired to his bed.

Having lost Ratnagiri to Mahisasura
The goddesses sheltered on the summit of Vindhyagiri.

Sorry to see Durga moving in the sky as a homeless
Wanderer, Indra brought her a *khechari*
Chariot and requested her to use it. She took
Her seat in the chariot, Sanchaketu by name,
And, in the blink of an eye, she travelled
Over the seven islands and the whole universe.
The Creator offered her valuable gifts as
A sign of gratitude.'

Sage Shuka said, 'O King! Mahisasura
Was busy consulting Dhumralochana.
Impatient, he could not stay seated at one
Place. He was beating his arms and saying
Regretfully, "Why I didn't I fight the battle
Earlier? It was my misfortune that such
An idea didn't occur to me. I missed
The chance of killing the women with my own
Hands, and, unfortunately, got my friends
Killed, instead."

It became morning. The sound of conches
Filled the air. Leaving bed, Mahisa got up angrily,
A mace in his hand. After ablutions, he said
His prayers to Brahma and changed himself into
A fierce lion of enormous size that covered
The earth, as clouds cover the sky. He reached
Subarnachuda mountain, the present abode of Durga.
Panicked, the other goddesses left their carriers
And began to run. Durga consoled them, "Don't
Be scared. I'll kill Mahisasura now and fulfil
The promise I'd made to the gods."

Asking them to wait and see, she changed
Herself into a lion, of the size of Vindhyagiri.
And flew into the sky. When Durga and Mahisasura
Met each other, it looked like the Meru and the Mandara
Mountains placed close to each other. The earth
Shone with the radiance of both the lions.
They banged their heads against each other
Which rocked the earth and deafened the three worlds.
They scratched each other with their claws;
The blood flowing from the wounds they had
Received looked like the rising moon. Their mouths
Hanging open seemed to swallow the three worlds.
The gods, in fear, fled their abode. Their feet
Covered the netherworld and heaven, their ears
Looked as big as the universe. Their bodies were
Impenetrable and their chests looked like
Mountains made of iron. When they breathed out,
The world seemed to flutter; the noise was like
That of a thunder cloud. The push of their
Bodies emitted a huge fire that seemed
To burn down the Creation. The battle continued
Throughout the day and the night, the moon
And the sun hiding themselves in the sea.
There was no day, no night, no sun, no moon.
The radiance of their bodies was the only
Source of light. The nine kingdoms comprising
The earth shook in fear. In absence of air,
All living beings lay lifeless. At the time
Goddess Durga pounced on Mahisasura's
Chest and tried to tear it with her claws,
Teeth and in many other ways, but it was all

In vain. Having failed in her attempt to hurt
Him, she sat where she was and told him,
"I must thank you, O Mahisasura, for your
Unflinching devotion to Brahma who was
Pleased to give you a boon that made your
Body as stiff as thunder. I'm surprised,
You look exactly like the lion I use as
My carrier." So saying, the merciful Goddess
Let go of him.

Leaving the battle, Mahisasura, scurried away.
Completely worn out. As the sun rose, his
Disguise fell off and he returned to his former
Self. When he entered the palace, his queens, Kali
And Karali, came out to welcome him. Broken down
With shame and exertion, he had no followers with
Him to whom he could confide the details. Sorry
To find him in a deplorable state, his queens suggested,
"Let's go and surrender to the woman without
A second thought. Tying an axe around our necks
And a straw between our teeth, we'll beg her for
Forgiveness." Feeling a bit relieved, he sat calmly.
In an attempt to ease his agony,
He carried on a dialogue with himself,
"If I take the path of righteousness
And beg pardon of her, it will be an insult to
The demon clan. As far as I know she is a ruthless
Woman. I don't expect kindness from her at all.
A woman is the most stupid of all living beings.
How can she behave respectfully? I'm sure she'll
Never forgive me and spare my life, either.
What shall I gain by sitting idle, doing nothing?

That'll be disgrace to the demon community."
While he was brooding over those thoughts, Sindhu
And Upasindhu reached there.

With bears as their carriers and ten lakh soldiers
At their command, they were the commanders
Of Mahisasura, stationed at Yojanagiri.
The *chandals*, who used to guard the city at night,
Heard the king's wailing while travelling through
The city. Puzzled, they met the king, and, with
Consolatory words, tried to comfort him. Being
Heavily drunk, they forgot how and what to speak
To the king. Sindhu and Upasindhu reached the king
Soon after, and, with due respect, told him,
"Why do you worry when we're there to protect
You? You've taken care of so long. If we don't
Stand by you now, of what use are we, then?
O Lord! We take the vow that we'll kill the women
And leave no trace of them." Happy to hear this,
Mahisasura felt that all was not lost; there was
Still a ray of hope for him. He offered them
Finery, plenty of gems and ornaments.
He addressed them as benignly as a slave would
Do, "My sons! If you save my clan, which is
Now under the threat of extinction, your fame
Will spread throughout the ages." Moved by the king's
Words, the commanders proceeded southwards
With their troops, among the sound of the marching
Band. Having one leg and eight hands each,
They were armed with mace, *konta* and sword.
With two lakh soldiers, Dhakasura marched
To Ratnagiri; Bhaksha was dispatched to Vindhyagiri

With two lakh soldiers, and Sindhu, with the rest
Of soldiers, kept guard over the area to
The south of the mountain.

Feeling a surge of danger,
The Goddess asked Chandramukhi to go with
Four lakh *betalas* to check the number of the demons
And to find out if Mahisasura was present among
Them. The *betali*, standing on the summit of
The mountain, cast her eyes around. Returning,
She reported that Mahisasura was not there,
And that Sindhu and Upasindhu, the commanders
In charge of the city, were leading the troops. Hearing
This, the Goddess called Kothari, Ugratara, Kola Ambika,
Nimanjai and Tripura and told them, "The five of you
Battle with the demons and finish them off." With
Swords in hands, they flew into the sky. Seeing
The vast army, looking like the sea, they were scared,
Like snakes facing Garuda. They raised a war
Cry that deafened the world. The battle broke out,
The demons firing arrows at them incessantly.
But their arrows were burnt into ashes by the fire
From the eyes of the goddesses. They knifed into
The battlefield, and, groping among the demons,
They tore the bodies of many warriors into shreds.
They pulled their ears. They wrung the necks
Of many of the demons and made their heads
Into a garland. They wore it around their necks
And went wild. The demons continued hitting
Their heads with maces again and again,
But their weapons were destroyed as grass by
Fire. With no weapons, the demons started landing

Blows and slaps on the goddesses. But how could
They harm them with their hands when their weapons
Failed to do so? The red-looking goddesses, dancing, pushed
Their mouths into the wounds of the demons went on
Drinking their blood. Holding them by the legs, they
Tossed them into the air and swallowed them as they
Fell. Stark naked, they sang, danced and ululated
While devouring the demons. Too mysterious were
Their ways to be explained.'

Those who listen to the story of Chandi's war
Face no hardship in their lives. It is both entertaining
And educative. I bow to Durga who fulfils all
The wishes and blesses her devotees with wealth
And children. Most gratefully, I bow at her
Lotus-feet hundred and thousands of times,
Says Sudramuni Sarala Das.

x x x

Abhimanyu's son told the sage, 'The four
Ideals that constitute a righteous life are
Dharma, *artha*, *kama* and *moksha*. You're Brahman,
You only can show me the path to righteousness.
The sins I committed, knowingly or unknowingly,
Are washed away by the river of your words which
Are no less than nectar. O Sage!
Now tell me about how Mahisasura was killed.'
Shuka explained:

'The ten lakh warriors engaged in the battle
With the goddesses were at last killed and devoured.
The goddesses chopped their bodies with swords

And arrows and ate their bones and flesh. Seeing
Sindhu and Upasindhu, Durga, in anger, rushed
Towards them, but was prevented by Ugratara
And Tripura from proceeding further. They
Volunteered to take on the demons themselves.
They moved forward to the demon commanders,
Seated in chariots to which four thousand
Donkeys were yoked. They opened their mouths,
The upper lip raised to the height of the mountain
And the lower lip touching the earth. They swallowed
The chariots, each measuring an area of nine
Thousand hands. Leaving the chariots, Sindhu
And Upasindhu hurried to the goddesses
And struck their heads with their maces, as
Huge as mountains. But, instead of causing
Any harm to the goddesses, the maces were crushed
To powder. Ugratara chopped their heads off
With a cutlass, but as soon as their heads
Fell off, new heads sprung from their trunks.
Rising to their feet, the demons launched an
Assault on the goddesses again, who cut-off
Their heads as before, which were soon replaced.
The goddesses were in a fix when Chetani,
A Goddess, appeared before them and said,
"Don't be brittle. These demons are
The grandsons of Japasura, a great *yogi*,
Who is now meditating on the Ranastambha
Mountain. He worships Wind-god, offering
Him food every day. While in meditation,
Japasura sits, stretching his hands forward,
Whatever falls on his hands, he eats it up.
O Ugratara! You can eliminate them only if

You do as I say. Collect Lord Shiva's trident,
Brahma's arrow and Indra's thunder.
Shoot them from the *ajagaba* bow at the demons.
The arrows will fly them to Japasura, who'll
Swallow them immediately. Aim the trident
At their navels, thunder at their chest
And Brahma's arrow at their throats.
This is the secret of their death."

Tripura and Ugratara prayed to
Brahma, Shiva and Indra who offered
Them the arrow, the trident and the thunder.
When Ugratara fitted the weapons to the *ajagaba*
Bow, the Sun, terrified, left the sky. The Earth,
The Water, the Fire, the Wind and the Sky froze
In fear. Suddenly the voice of Providence was heard
From above: "O Mother! Take care that
The weapons hit the demons and not fall on
The earth, which may be disastrous for the creation."
Taking all precautions, the Goddess fired
The weapons at the demons which pierced into
Their bodies and flew them into Japasura's
Hands. Japasura, faint with hunger, swallowed
Them instantly. That's how the lives of Sindhu
And Upasindhu came to an end. The gods
In heaven rejoiced at their death.'

Glory to Tripura,
The story of whose heroic deeds is endless!
When Brahma fails to explain her greatness,
How can I, being a man, do it?
By pleasing her, one can be redeemed

Of one's fear of death.
Sudramuni Sarala Das prays at her lotus-feet.

x x x

'Too shocked to hear that Sindhu and Upasindhu
Are now no more, Mahisasura broke down. Remembering
All that had happened in the recent past, he bewailed,
"Of what use is my life now? I'll surely take poison
And die. I'd one hundred *padmas* of warriors, the most
Formidable on the earth and in the netherworld.
I'd one crore *kshaunis* of foot soldiers. All had
Lost their lives in the fourteen-day battle. Now
There is no trace of any of them who once ruled
The whole world. How many of my great friends
Didn't I lose in the battle! What is left for me
To do in this world? Surely, I'll lay down my life
In today's battle. As long as my sinful soul exists,
My worry would keep growing day by day. If I'm
Fated to die one day, why not today?" Coming
Out of the palace, he commanded Dhumralochana
To get the chariot ready. Dhumralochana
Fitted the Sanchaketu chariot with precious
Jewels which Mahisa had plundered from heaven.
That beautiful chariot needed no carriers
And it flew at the whim of the charioteer.

Mahisasura adorned himself with
The Biraketana crown studded with diamond
And emerald; beads of diamonds and gems
Hanging from it covered his forehead. He wore
Earrings of gems and pearls that hung over
His cheeks. He put on four rounds of a necklace

Around his neck, armlets and bracelets studded
With gems and diamonds, rings made of
Eight kinds of gems on his fingers and bejewelled
Anklets. He held a bow with clusters of gems
And pearls fitted to its ends and golden bells
Hanging from it. It was a rare bow, Kushaketu
By name, offered to him by Brahma after
His conquest of heaven. That bow, which looked
More beautiful than the Mekhalagiri, he held
In his left hand. He filled the quiver with
Five crore arrows made of Jatayu's wings
And studded with gems. He stowed one thousand
Guruja and five thousand swords in the chariot.
Finally he put on the armour. All this made him
Look like the rising sun.

O Parikshit! When the monarch
Of the world got into the chariot, the sky
Turned grey; hot wind blew from the north
And the earth felt like burning. It was
The eighth day of the bright fortnight of Ashwin,
On which the stars were all placed, which was
An inauspicious sign for a journey to the south.
Dhumralochana drove the chariot southwards,
With the king, looking like a livid flame, inside.
The chariot flew at the speed of the wind;
In a few moments it reached Ratnagiri.
Narayani informed Durga about Mahisasura
Arriving in a chariot, unaccompanied.
Anticipating attack from his side, Durga got
Into her *khechari* chariot and flew into the sky.
On the banks of Ganga they met each other.

Listen, O King! Amazed by Durga's beauty,
Mahisasura asked her sternly, "Where did you
Come from, hey strange woman? Seducing
My friends by sweet words, you took their lives.
How treacherous and cruel a woman can be!
I'll cook your flesh and eat it. I'll bathe with
Your blood and avenge the death of my friends."
The Goddess replied in a harsh voice, "O the Foe
Of the gods! What right do you have to live
After letting all your friends die? O boastful
Demon! I'll cut you into pieces. I'll send you
To Yama's abode to be eaten by vultures
And jackals." Infuriated, Kapilasingha's son
Took the bow and shot one thousand arrows
At her one thousand hands. At this, Durga
Retaliated by firing arrows at him. The demon
Sent two thousand arrows, then nine lakhs
That covered the sky, but all of those were
Burnt down by the glint of her eyes.
The exchange of arrows darkened the sky
And fell to the ground like the rains of Shravana.

Failing in his attempt to defeat Durga,
Mahisasura used the arrows he had received
From the gods. First, he fired a *parbata*
Arrow which rained down stones and boulders
On her chariot. Some of them were one *yojana*
Long. In reply, Durga shot a *bajrabali*
Arrow that broke the stones into small pieces.
Then, she sent the *Agni* arrow, challenging Mahisa
To destroy it. Surprised by her prowess in
Archery, Bajrasingha's grandson asked her,

"O great woman! Where did you learn these
Wonderful skills from? Never have I seen
A woman, such as you, who routed the great
Army of mine. Who says women are weaklings?
Had I known your attributes earlier, I would
Have surrendered to you and learnt many
Things from you. Now, listen to me. Be my wife.
See, if you kill me, you'll achieve nothing.
But, if I kill you, I'll be famous in the three
Worlds. I swear, I'll remain faithful to you
Forever. Please have mercy on me." Durga
Replied, "You needn't ask for my mercy.
In the battle between the two clans, the gods
And the demons, there is least chance of your
Survival. I could have saved you hadn't you been
So cruel to the gods. You tormented them, depriving
Them of their rights. I've no other option than
Killing you to restore peace and order in heaven."

Taking offence, Mahisasura hissed like
An angry cobra. *Agni* arrow sent by her
Was destroyed as it reached Dhumralochana.
Mahisa shot at her the *Ahi* arrow that stung
The Goddess causing immense pain. In response,
She fired the *garuda* arrow that swallowed
Mahisa's arrow. Then, she shot the *nirghanta*
Arrow which Dhumralochana caught with
His left hand. In anger, Mahisasura fired
The *megha* arrow that caused a heavy rainfall.
Which Durga paid back with *rudra* arrow
That stopped the rain. The *Brahma* arrow Durga
Shot next was broken into pieces by Dhumralochana.

Annoyed with Dhumralochana's interference,
She let out a roar of rage from which
Two demonesses, Kankasuni and Lomasuni, were
Born. Their upper lips touched the sky and the nether
Lips the earth. Durga commanded them,
"Swallow Dhumralochana and the Sanchaketu
Chariot so that, I can have a full view
Of Mahisasura." With folded hands, Kankasuni
Said, "I'll take on Dhumralochana." Lomasuni
Said, "I'll swallow the chariot." Both flew into
The sky and rushed towards Mahisasura
Who shot arrows at them to prevent them from
Advancing. Kankasuni swallowed the arrows,
And, with them, Dhumralochana too. Next
She gulped the Sanchaketu chariot. Scared,
Mahisasura disappeared from there. With her
Divine eyes, Durga discovered him in the sky.
Alighting from her chariot, she rode her lion
And reached Mahisasura. Seeing her, the demon
Launched an attack on her with bow and arrow.
The exchange of arrows and jangling of maces
Continued, neither side showing any sign
Of defeat. The demon's *chakunda* arrow was
Destroyed by Durga's *rudra* arrow and his
Kalachakra by the Goddess's *baruna* arrow.
When all his weapons were destroyed, Mahisa
Changed himself into a huge buffalo, his body
Occupying the whole of the Jambu island.
The bejewelled buffalo looked as shining as
The Udayagiri. The Goddess rained down
Arrows on him incessantly, but none of them
Could pierce into his body. The buffalo stood

As firm as the Meru mountain, looking radiant.
Even Durga's divine weapons did not work.
Mahisa, then, charged at the lion with his
Horns. Durga told the lion, "You take on
The buffalo. I've taken a vow to kill Mahisasura."
She struck him with mace and trident again
And again, but it was all in vain. She,
At last, shot at him the *Kopanala* arrow, the most
Fatal of all her weapons. But Mahisa caught
It with his left hand. Infuriated, Durga struck
His shoulders with a cutlass that severed
His head from his body which fell to the
Ground. The earth shook violently, as if
The Mandaragiri had given way, while the gods
Cheered and strew gold on the Goddess.

As the buffalo's head was chopped off,
Mahisa came out from inside its body like the sun
Rising. He had a *parigha* in his left hand
And a dagger in the right. The Goddess struck
His chest with a trident, and, standing on him,
Pressed one of her feet on his cheek. Soon she was
Joined by nine crore Katyayanis, fifty-six crore
Pichasunis, sixty-four *yoginis*, nine *marbhuta*
Sronehas, three *padma* Chandis, fourteen crore
Dakinis, fifty-six crore Chamundis, seven *sagara*
Goddesses, some of whom were Ugratara, Chandi,
Kothari, Golama, Marakama, Yamakama, Maheswari,
Kali, Kankali, Betali, Bhairabi and Kankasuni,
Eighteen crore Rudrayanis and fifty-two crore
Brahmayanis. All of them pounced on Mahisa.
The nine crore Katyayanis sat on his chest,

The sixty-four *yoginis* pushed the trident into
His body, the hundred *marbhuta* Kamarupis
Held his hands firmly, five *padma dakinis*
Held his thighs, one hundred *pichasunis* caught
Hold of his body, fifty-six crore goddesses
Held Mahisa's four legs and fourteen crore
Bhairabis wrung his neck. Thirty-three crore
Goddesses ate the flesh from his back
And the lion gnawed at his chest.

Incensed, Mahisa shook his body with
A jerk that threw the goddesses to far-off
Places. One lakh crore fell in Padma island,
Fourteen crore Bhairabis in Chandra island,
Nine *padma* Chandis in Kusha island, three
Hundred crore Chamandis in Karancha island,
Hundred *padma pichasunis* in Padma island,
Fourteen crore demonesses in the Milky Sea,
Nine core Katyayanis in Jambu island, one
Padma dakinis and sixty-four *yoginis* in
The forest who later became forest deities.
Durga was left alone, her companions thrown
Afar, immobile. Some of them lost their eyes
And were mained, others fractured their
Bones. All of them turned to stone wherever
They lay. They were worshipped as goddesses
Later. Seizing the opportunity, Mahisa slipped into
The deep sea. Durga followed him into the deep
Sea and pressed his chest with her feet not
To let go of him. She knew once he escaped,
He would destroy the three worlds. All living beings
Would perish. Just then, the voice of Providence

Was heard from above: "Never let him go;
Hold him down. Once he escapes, he will never
Be killed. O Merciful Goddess! We pray to you
Not to let us down." The concern of the gods
Touched her. She produced a Goddess from her
Body, who had four hands, four faces and red
Complexion. She was dressed in white and sitting
On a lotus, two of her hands were in the pose
Of blessing. Durga asked her, "I failed to kill
The demon who is hiding in the sea. Where did
You come from?" She replied, "I was born
To you. Don't fret. Once you let go of the demon,
He'll devour the gods in a moment. O Mother!
I was inside you. Moved by your bitter agony,
I came out." Durga told her, "O my daughter!
I seek your help to finish off Mahisasura."
Realizing her mother's anxiety, she hurled a snare
Into the sea and caught him. Then she pulled
It hard and brought both Durga and the demon
Ashore. There was a kingdom called Kashi nearby
Where they laid the demon and held him down.
But Mahisasura was trying hard to break
Loose from them and escape into the sky.
The Goddess, seated on the lotus, told Durga,
"Listen, mother, to the story of Mahisasura's
Past. In Satya Yuga, he meditated on Brahma
For one lakh sixty thousand years. Pleased
With his devotion, Brahma offered him a boon.
He told him, 'Grant me the boon that no man
Can kill me and that I can defeat Vishnu
In war.' Andhaka, his minister, warned him that
He might be killed by a woman, if not by man.

Mahisa scolded him for his stupid remark,
Since he thought women were too weak and too
Foolish to dare him. The minister insisted,
'Don't forget that Narayana takes feminine
Form to kill the demons.' Greatly worried,
Mahisa begged Brahma, 'In case a woman
Kills me, bless me that I'll die watching her
Naked form.' O Mother! You've to prepare
Yourself accordingly. Unless he sees your
Genitals, he is not going to die now or ever.
So, mother, take off your clothes and ensure
The death of the wicked demon." Bewildered,
Durga exclaimed, "What a shame to expose
My nakedness to everyone!" The Goddess, sitting
On the lotus, told her, "If that's your worry,
How can the three worlds be saved? That he is
Still alive is because the secret of his death
Was not known." Just then, the gods sounded
Out: "O Durga! What she says is right."
She reminded Durga, "What about your promise
To the gods, that you'll destroy the demon?
If you don't keep your words, you betray
The gods who relied on you. After you were born,
You stretched your hands towards them and they
Equipped you with their weapons. You also took
A vow to kill the demon. They have been waiting
Long to see you act. If you disappoint them,
You'll be blamed. O Mother! The sun may rise
In the west; the ocean may overflow the north
Shore, lotuses may bloom on the mountain,
But great men never falter in their commitment.
Unable to bear with the humiliations by the demons,

The gods had sought your support." So saying,
She bowed at her feet in respect.'

Glory to you, O Katyayani, the Merciful,
The Protector of mankind! Chanting your name,
One leads a life, healthy and hearty.
The Goddess who was born to Durga will remove
The obstacles in your life. She has no beginning
Nor end. Think on her; she will bless you with
Wisdom. Sudramuni Sarala Das owes whatever
Achievements he has to her.

Shuka said, 'That Goddess tipped off Durga
How to kill Mahisasura. It was too difficult
To hold him back for a long time. Suddenly
He got up and ran at the speed of the wind.
The Goddess cautioned Durga, "Take off your
Clothes and follow him before it is too late."
Durga protested, "Isn't it embarrassing to do
As you say? How can I commit a sin, the like
Of which is never seen, nor heard of, for
The sake of killing a despicable demon?
Let not the wicked demon die; let the gods
Be driven away from heaven; let the nine
Islands of the world be destroyed. But I can't
Show my naked body to the three worlds."

Mahisasura, breaking out of the place,
Ran on and on until he reached the Kameka
Forest on the bank of River Tarini.
Time was running out and the demon was
Slipping away. Without a second thought,

Durga took the form of Chamunda. She removed
All her clothes except a little piece of cloth
That covered her genitals. She wore her hair
Loose, and her thighs and breasts were bare.

Stunned to see her stark naked,
Mahisasura mused, "Bless my soul! I consider
It my good fortune to see the rarest of the rare
Sight that the gods can never expect to see.
As they could not kill me in war, they are now
Using a woman as a decoy. This was, of course,
What I wished for, otherwise the whole creation
Would have been in peril. Didn't I wish to see,
The genitals of the woman who would kill me?"
He lay on the bank of Tarini river, left
Completely drained. Durga stood
On him, one of her feet on his chest. His eyes
Locked on her genitals, he breathed his last.

Expressing her gratitude to her daughter,
Durga said, "I'd given birth to many Chandis,
But you're the best of all. I name you as
Sarbamangala. You protected the gods from
An imminent disaster. You'll also protect
The mankind against evils." O Parikshit!
Durga asked Ratnagiri to trample Mahisasura's
Dead body. Before leaving the place for heaven,
She called out to her companions, such as
Narayani, Indrayani, Rudrayani, Bhairabi,
Brahmayani, Baseli, Chachika, Madhabi, Kali,
Kankali, Betali, Ugratara, Samadi, Matangi,
Chandika, Tripura, Ramachandi, Nimanjai,

Shyanti, Marakama, Kothari, Ambika, Eloma,
Golama, Bhataleka, Kalama, Rupa, Birupa,
Shyma, Subhanti, Nisabali, Binjhabali,
Aniti, Pakheni, Sarangi, Champai, Rupai, Jamai,
Barunai, Pichikai, Bahadai, Khudai, Soubhagi,
Saudai, Lemua, Kenduasuni, Andhari, Dakeni,
Hathibaseni, Sadhebi, Rudhi, Samuka, Sarabinda,
Nila, Kamala, Soneha, Makunda, Bhagita,
Munita, Utani, Nangana, Khepa, Mekhala,
Mahakhala, Ghoti, Bahani, Kamarupi,
Chandrama, Juhai, Tripura, Tarini, Sare,
Jatuali, Hingula, Charu, Chamandi, Bikala,
Bhadrakali, Jakshari, Sagari, Nirakuli,
Singhala, Barahi, Anantai, Sara, Dhvateswari,
And others, who were four *kharbas*
In number. They were accompanied by nine
Crore Katyayanis, five *padma pichasunis*,
And sixty-four *yoginis*. Durga commanded
All of them, "Rush to Jenabati city forthwith
And devour the demons and demonesses."
At this, the goddesses, like a flock of hawks,
Swooped on the city. They consumed the whole
Demon population – young and old – leaving
No trace of them.

O Parikshit! In the midnight
Of Thursday, the eighth day of Ashwin,
Mahisasura was killed. Durga was born
In the midnight of the bright fortnight
Of the eighth day of Ashwin. The same day
She arrived in Ratnagiri, riding a lion.
Beginning with that day, the battle continued

Until the eighth day of the next fortnight.
On the ninth day the demon community was
Completely wiped out.

On her arrival in heaven, the gods,
Exceedingly happy, worshipped her with
Many offerings. They requested her to give up
Her terrible form and return to her former self.
Lord Shiva, terrified, prayed to her benignly:

"You're my third eye. My life and death
Are in your hands. You're the creator; you're
Brahman. The Water, the Fire, the Wind and
The Sky are your manifestations.
You're the source of wisdom,
The essence of meditation and spiritual
Knowledge. You're *siddha*; you're *sadhu*.
You're the cause of sorrow and the redeemer
Of it. You're the ultimate goal of every soul.
You're the beginning of every thing. O Mother!
You symbolize the eternal joy. The greatest
Sages seek your blessings." So saying, the Lord
Bowed at her feet in respect.'

Durga is the Saviour and Well-wisher
Of mankind. She is the eternal flame of hope
And life. She represents *susumna*.
She is indestructible; she is Gayatri, she is
Death incarnate. She protects her devotees
Against all evils. Thus says Sarala Das,
Bowing at her lotus-feet.

x x x

Sage Shuka told the king:
'Terrified by the sight of Durga, all the gods
Made a hasty exit, except Lord Shiva, who,
Unable to escape, started singing and dancing
To please her. He was praying to her to save his life
And to have mercy on him. Seeing him so scared,
She took pity on him. "I'm pleased with your
Devotion," she said, "Tell me what you want.
I promise to fulfil your wish." The Lord replied,
"I know I am not worthy of your mercy. I beg
You for granting me a long life." She put one
Of her hands on his head and blessed him,
"You'll be immortal. You may ask for any
Other boon without fear." "I pray to you to put
Your clothes on," he implored. To which she said,
"Don't you know I've taken a vow not to cover
My body?" The Lord, then, said, "I wish to have
You as my wife." So saying, he moved past
Her, but she called after him, asking him to wait.
She went over and held his hand. Then,
She put a garland around his neck. She looked
Into his face and said, "You're naked, so am I.
We're now man and wife." Delighted, Shiva
Took her into his lap and held her in deep
Embrace. He spread his long-matted hair
Over her that covered her body completely,
Except for her face that shone like the moon.

Narada reported the whole story to Brahma,
"The Lord of Beasts and Durga are in love with
Each other. Pleased with his devotion, she offered
Him a boon. Shiva asked her to become his wife,

To which she consented. Now, Uma and Maheswar
Are united with each other." Hearing this,
Brahma, Indra, the Moon, the Sun, the Wind, Baruna
And others flocked to her. They bowed at her
Lotus-feet and expressed their gratitude to her.
When Brahma prayed to her with offerings,
She forbade him. Pointing at Sarbamangala,
She said, "This Goddess is the one who deserves
Your offerings. It is she who saved me from
Drowning and caught Mahisa with a snare
And brought him ashore. All other goddesses
Who had accompanied me were thrown away
By Mahisa in different directions. When
All my attempts to hold back Mahisa fell through
And I was trying hard to prevent him from
Escaping, this Goddess revealed to me the secret
Of Mahisasura's death. She told me the only way
To kill him was to strip off. She brought wind
To my sails which helped me to kill the demon.
She brought an end to the discontent and gloom
That had overtaken the three worlds."

O Parikshit!
I bow to Katyayani, the incarnation of Vishnu,
Who fulfils the wishes of one and all. Her
Reddish-blue complexion soothes every heart.
She is compassionate and merciful. Her glory
Is undying. She is the Saviour of mankind.
She is Aparna, as powerful as Time and Fire,
Who can make and unmake the destiny
Of the world. She is incomprehensible, fearless
And indomitable. She has no beginning,

Middle nor end. The story of her heroic deeds
Can never be put to words. How can I, being
A man, explain it? O the Wise! By worshipping
Her you can achieve everything in life –
Wealth, children, good health and security.

O the Wise! In the midnight of Tuesday,
The eighth day of the bright fortnight of Ashwin,
The Goddess had arrived in Ratnagiri. On
The eighth day of the dark fortnight Chanda
And Munda were killed. The battle lasted for
Sixteen days. In the night of the fifteenth day
Mahisasura was slain. On the ninth day
Of the bright fortnight of Ashwin, the demons
In Jenabati were wiped out. The next Thursday
Durga adorned Shiva's lap, which is
Considered the most auspicious
Day of the month.'

For Parikshit to be blessed with a son,
Sage Shuka held a *yajna* from which a child
Was born. The sage named him Janmejaya.
The hearing of the scripture bore fruit, it saved
Parikshit's Moon clan from extinction.
That was the benefit of listening to Chandika's
Story. Overwhelmed with joy, the king worshipped
At the feet of the sage, offering him finery,
Earrings and a garland of gems. He fell
At his feet with a pot filled with five crore gems.

O Noble ones!
Blessed are those who listen to Chandi's story.
They succeed in life and their sins, like

Water on a lotus leaf, do not affect their life.
Their fear of the wrath of the royal authority
Is redeemed and their bodies purified. How can
I describe her glory whom Brahma, Krupajal
By name, prays, seeking her blessings?
She is the one whom Parshurama, Renuka's son,
Worships by offering blood.

The goddess of Jankherpur will bring
An end to Kali Yuga herself or through others,
While she exists for all eternity. I owe all I have
To her. I'll act as her humble servant all
My life. I don't know how to chant, worship
And meditate. It is Sarala Chandi, the benevolent
Goddess, who imparted the spiritual knowledge
On me, even though I was mired in ignorance.
She dictates me what to write
And I put them into words. O the Wise!
Forgive me if you find any mistakes.

Thus says Sudramuni Sarala Das,
The poet, bowing at Sarala Chandi's feet.

Glossary

Aditya : the sun

ajagaba : also Ajanga, Pinaka; Lord Shiva's bow

Alakapuri : the abode of Kubera, the custodian of wealth in heaven

Amaravati : the abode of Indra, king of gods

Anakara : also Nirakara; God

Annapurna : the benevolent Goddess who provides food for all; Parvati

Aparna : Parvati; so called as she did not eat anything, not even a leaf (*parna*), during her meditation to have Shiva as her husband

Ardrabali : the rainbow

artha : wealth

bahutia : an animal of the deer family

Balaram's weapon : the plough

Baraswatipura : the abode of Indra

Barunapura : the abode of Baruna, God of Waters

betala : (feminine: *betali*) the followers of Lord Shiva

bharana : 80 gaunis, one gauni = 8 seers (approx.)

Bhusandakaka : Kakbhusundi in Sanskrit; a crow named Bhusanda who was cursed by Sage Lomasa. Anticipating its death, it flew to Sri Jagannath Temple, Puri, where it fell into the Rohinikunda and got salvation by turning into four-armed Vishnu

bimba : a creeper; its fruit looks shining red when it is ripe

brahmachari : one who practises continence and studies the Vedas in the preceptor's house after investiture

Brahman : the ultimate reality underlying all phenomena

brahmarsi : a brahmin who becomes a sage

brahmasara : a very powerful and lustrous weapon (arrow); Guru Dronacharya learnt its use from Agasti and taught it to Arjuna and Aswastthama

brunda : 1,000 crore

chakora : also *chakrobaka*; a bird said to be living on moonlight

chamara : cowrie; a long brush made of tufts of the tail-hair of an yak, used as a fan or a fly-whisk

chandal : a low born

Chandi : Goddess Durga

Dadhibamana : also Dadhimangala; Vishnu; the *Bamana Purana* mentions Vishnu carrying curd (*dadhi*) during his incarnation as Bamana (the dwarf)

dakini : a follower of Goddess Kali

Daksha : one of Brahma's sons and the progenitor of mankind

dambaru : a small double-faced drum in the shape of an hour-glass, associated with Lord Shiva

Damodara : Vishnu

danda : 24 minutes

dikpalas : the gods ruling the ten directions. According to Manu, they are Kubera, Indra, Bayu, Yama, Baruna, Agni, the Moon, the Sun, Brahma and Vishnu. The Vedas mention five *dikpalas* and the Buddhists four

Durga : the Goddess who killed Mahisasura. The ten forms of Durga are Kali, Tara, Sodashi, Bhubaneswari, Bhairabi, Chhinnamasta, Dhumabati, Bagala, Matangi and Kamala. In *Durga Saptasati*, they are Shailaputri, Brahmacharini, Chandraghanta, Kusmanda, Skandamata, Katyayani, Kalaratri, Mahagauri and Siddhidatri

gandharvas : also *vidyadharas*; demi-gods, whose wives are called *apsaras*

gauri and *sauri* : a method of cooking in which vegetables are not chopped, nor spices added

Gayatri : the most powerful Vedic *mantra*; the mother of the four Vedas

Girija : Parvati; so called as she was the daughter of a mountain (*giri*), the Himalayas

Garuda : a huge mythical bird born to Kashyap and Binata. He was a great Vaishnava and the carrier of Vishnu

garuda : a weapon resembling a mace

Harivamsa : *Harivamsa Purana* written by Vyasa; another Sanskrit version by Jinasena (AD 783) and Odia version by Achyutananda Das

Hemavanta : the Himalayas

Hemavantapura : the abode of Lord Shiva

Hiranyagarvapura : the abode of the Sun

Jambu island : one of the nine islands in which India is situated

Jatayu : king of vultures; son of Aruna and Syeni in the *Mahabharata* and son of Garuda in the *Ramayana*

Kalapurusa : the messenger of death; the son of the Sun who has six heads, sixteen hands, twenty-four eyes and six feet. He is dark in complexion and dressed in red

Kama : God of Love. Some of his other names are Mara, Kandarpa, Manasija, Madana, Pradyumna, Makaradhwaja, Minaketan and Darpaka

kamandalu : also *kamandal*; an oblong-shaped water-pot used by ascetics

Kamyak : a forest on the banks of River Saraswati; Sage Gautam lived there

Kapila : son of Sage Kadama and Debahuti; the fifth incarnation of God; the propounder of the Sankhya philosophy

Kartik : also Karttikeya, Kumara and Skanda; Lord Shiva's son

Kashyap : so named as he had the complexion of *kasha* flower; the son of Maruchi and grandson of Brahma; the composer of many *shlokas* of *Rigveda*

kharba	: 10,000 crore
khatwang	: a long, studded club used as a weapon
khechari	: a yogic exercise in which the attention of the *yogi* is focused on the space between the eyebrows
kinnara	: singers of heaven with bodies of men and heads of horses
konta	: a weapon
kshetrapala	: God worshipped at the border of a place of pilgrimage
kshauni	: 10,00,000×10,000,000 crore
kumkum	: a red cosmetic powder or paste
lita	: 60 *lita* =1 *danda* = 24 seconds
Maheswari	: Durga
Managovinda	: Duryodhana
mandapa	: a platform which is open on all sides; usually attached to a temple
Mandara	: a huge mountain; it was used for churning the sea by the gods and the demons
marbhuta	: 10 crore
Matali	: Lord Indra's charioteer
maya	: illusion
medha	: also *madha*; 1 *madha* = 0.8 grams
Meru	: the Meru mountain of mythological fame; also called Sumeru, Hemadri, Ratnasanu, Amaradri, etc. It is 84,000 *yojana* in height, of which 16,000 *yojana* are submerged by the sea. It has three mounts. It finds a mention in the *Bhagavata*, the *Nrisimha Purana* and the *Kurma Purana*. In modern geography, it is the North Pole, located in the Arctic circle

moksha	: salvation
naga	: cobra
Nahusa	: son of King Yayati
Narasimha	: the fourth incarnation of Vishnu who killed Hiranyakashyapa
nauti	: one *nauti* = 20 *gaunis*
Oda rastra	: the coastal districts of modern Odisha
padma	: 1 padma=1000000000000
Panchali	: Draupadi of the *Mahabharata*
parigha	: a weapon
Parikshit	: son of Abhimanyu and grandson of Arjuna, the third Pandava
pichasuni	: followers of Chandi
Prayag	: one of the holiest places in India
Raktabirjya	: Raktabija in Sanskrit
sagara	: 1 sagara = 10000000000000
Sampad	: also Sampati; Aruna's son and Jatayu's elder brother
Sanaka	: Brahma's son
Sanjibanipura	: the abode of Yama, King of Death
Shuka	: son of Vyasa and grandson of Parasara
sroneha	: bloodthirsty demi-goddesses
Sudramuni	: a saint among the sudras
Suravi	: the cow-Goddess; three primary *nadis* (channels of energy) of the human body related to yogic exercises
swayambara	: a form of marriage in which the bride chooses her husband from among the assembled suitors
tala	: length equal to a man's height
tandaba	: a terrible dance form performed by Shiva (Nagaraj), which brings destruction

tulsi	: basil plant
uluka vidya	: the art of making oneself invisible or taking various forms
Vishnu Purana	: written by Sage Parasara; it has 23,000 *shlokas* and it deals with the genesis
yajna	: sacrificial rites as enjoined by the Vedas
Yashobantipura	: the abode of Brahma
yojana	: 8 miles approximately